Changing the Subject
in English Class

Marshall W. Alcorn Jr.

Changing the Subject
in English Class

Discourse and the Constructions of Desire

Southern Illinois
University Press
CARBONDALE
AND EDWARDSVILLE

Publication partially funded by a subvention grant
from George Washington University.

An earlier version of chapter 2 was originally published as
"Changing the Subject of Postmodernist Theory:
Discourse, Ideology, and Therapy in the Classroom"
(*Rhetoric Review* 13 [1995]: 331–49)
and is used here with the permission of
Lawrence Erlbaum Associates.

Library of Congress Cataloging-in-Publication Data

Alcorn, Marshall W., 1949–
Changing the subject in English class : discourse and the constructions of desire / Marshall
W. Alcorn, Jr.
    p. cm.
  Includes bibliographical references (p.) and index.
    1. English language—Rhetoric—Study and teaching—United States. 2. English language—
Rhetoric—Study and teaching—Psychological aspects. 3. English language—Rhetoric—
Study and teaching—Political aspects. 4. English philology—Study and teaching
(Higher)—United States. 5. Language and culture—United States—History—20th century.
6. Report writing—Study and teaching (Higher)—United States. 7. Culture—Study and
teaching (Higher)—United States. 8. English language—Discourse analysis. I. Title.

PE1405.U6 A43 2002
808'.042'071073—dc21
ISBN 0-8093-2427-X (alk. paper)   2001020888

For my father,
Marshall Wise Alcorn,
and the memory of my mother,
Maxine Gertrude Langston,
and my stepmother,
Jewel Patrick Jordan

Contents

Preface

I would like to see an account of rhetoric that could imagine an American student's anxious half-thought about race in the classroom as a significant event in the context of some larger web of human communication, where in response to this half-thought, there are global implications for legal arguments about justice in Indonesia. This book does not go so far as to map out this ideal model for rhetoric, but it is an attempt to indicate relations between subtle movements of half-repressed feeling and larger movements of social action. To indicate some possibilities for this vision of rhetoric, I draw on the intellectual resources of postmodernist theory and psychoanalytic theory. I have labored to write a book that is readable, though it has not been an easy task. There are ever so many other finer discriminations that can and should be made for this argument. I have tried, though, to stay focused on the big picture, to formulate clear generalizations that make sense and to employ concrete examples that can support my claims. My desire for clarity, however, is threatened at every sentence. I am working with Lacanian theory, notorious for its density and paradox, as well as its failure as a systematic body of thought. I am also working with composition theory, notorious for its interdisciplinary range and lack of foundation. With the introduction of theory into literary studies twenty years ago, and its introduction into composition more recently, I fear we are no longer a community of scholars but a collection of different tribes with different dialects and tribal leaders. I have tried to write this book not for my tribe, Lacanians, but for others as well. I am trying to address very complicated material and I have a scope that may be a bit too broad to be proper for traditional scholarship. But I want to offer a big picture of what we do as teachers. I have tried to work with a limited set of well-defined concepts, and I have tried to speak with a personal voice.

I suspect that, despite my efforts, much of what I say will be dismissed as jargon by some. To the extent this book makes some sense, that small degree of clarity is owed primarily to my old friend, Mark Bracher. Years ago, Mark helped me (as a graduate student) to write a publishable paper by teaching me to work with a thesis statement and clear topic sentences.

I was not an English major as an undergraduate, and I had never learned the fine points of writing, though I had always done well with graduate papers. Twenty years have passed, and Mark continues to help as a reader; he responded carefully to a draft of this current manuscript (at a time when I myself was about to give up on it) and indicated how to make deletions and connections that would allow me to think of a jumbled collection of arguments as a book. I very much appreciate all the help over all the years.

I also want to thank James Berlin for responding kindly and generously to the *Rhetoric Review* article I wrote back in 1994 that became the ground of the argument for this book. I had attacked Berlin then for an oversimple understanding of subjectivity, and rather than dismissing my own argument as stupid, Berlin wanted to learn more. It was with great regret that I learned of his death. While I disagree with Berlin on many issues, I hope that this book helps to deepen and sharpen the arguments he makes regarding composition and ideology.

I have written on psychoanalysis for over twenty years, and I owe many people deep thanks for their patience and generosity in helping me to better understand material that is often paradoxical and hostile to easy assimilation. For the last ten years, I have met monthly with the Washington Lacan Reading Group, whose members have included Rick Boothby, Pat Crowe, Wilfried Ver Eecke, Macario Giraldo, Robert Samuels, Joe Smith, and Chris Venner. I have also been helped by two prominent Lacanian scholars who have taught at George Washington University, Robert Samuels and Renata Salcel. An enormous debt also goes to members of our George Washington University Lacan/Žižek Reading Group, scholars and graduate students (some now gone to new jobs) who have met happily over many years, including Clarissa Adamson, Tom Catlaw, Karen Coats, Macario Giraldo, Joe Smith, Cynthia McSwain, Rossitsa Terzieva, Bob Samuels, Evelyn Schreiber, Pier Stukes, Wilfried Ver Eecke, and Orion White.

At the same time that I have studied psychoanalysis, I have taught writing. My dissertation was on modern British literature, but like many scholars of my generation, I taught writing classes in temporary positions for many years. I learned to teach writing from James Kinneavy at the University of Texas in 1976, and after I received my PhD, I taught four courses of freshman writing each semester for three years at Texas. After my first son was born, I taught for a year at Iowa State University, and later, for three years, at Tulane University. When my second son was born, I took my first tenure-track job at Northern Illinois University, and after one year there, I moved to George Washington University, where I have taught freshman courses, advanced courses, and graduate courses in writing for over ten years. To all the faculty and staff at all these schools, I owe thanks.

A number of friends have helped me enormously with this manuscript. Karl Kageff has been a particularly kind and efficient editor at Southern Illinois University Press. Mark Bracher read the entire manuscript and offered copious suggestions. Jean Wyatt read chapter 5 carefully and offered smart criticism and encouragement. Victor Vitanza read much of chapter 4 as an prospective article for *PRE/TEXT* and offered insightful response. Jeff Berman read a draft of the book while finishing his own most recent work, *Risky Writing.* I feel a great debt to my wife and sons who have helped me understand the daily rhythm of speech, whereby desire is generated and circulated by social dialectic. Janis, Sean, and Skye, thank you.

Changing the Subject
in English Class

I Introduction

My title, *Changing the Subject in English Class*, suggests, I hope, two meanings. On the one hand, I want to talk about the shift in subject matter in English departments over the last twenty years. More and more teachers are teaching something generally called *cultural studies*, whereas before they had taught something generally called *literature* or *writing*. Literature, whatever the nature of that selected textuality, was taught as if it contained complex and accurate representations of human experience. The textual products of writing class were accepted as not so finely crafted, but they, too, were seen in a similar manner. Student writing expressed human experience, and teachers typically sought to help students in the accurate and complex representations of that experience. Now, however, as cultural studies promises to be the "subject" that unites the old division between literature and writing, it offers as its subject not the data of human experience but a method of decoding texts.

Cultural studies, however its texts are selected, is taught as a method to explore the movement and expression of a culture. In this sense, even though the actual books teachers use may not change, there has been a general shift in the subject taught in English. Even people who are teaching exactly the same texts as they did thirty years ago are often, in fact, teaching very different subjects. Texts, both literary and personal, do not contain human experience: they are instead evidence for the ideological work of culture. The new subject of English classes thus becomes culture, or perhaps for some teachers, ideology. Classroom work examines the work of culture or ideology, and this work is seen as contributing to political progress.

In a second sense of the term, I want to talk about a shift not in the subject that is taught but in the goals of teaching. In changing the subject matter that they teach, teachers increasingly also hope to change their students. They see their teaching in political terms; they want to change the world, and this means that they want to change the subjectivity of their students. In doing cultural studies, many teachers want to make their students more politically responsible, more in dialogue with the great social movements that dominate our time. Thus, the subjectivity of the student becomes a subject that the method of cultural studies works on as it responds to the subject matter of a text.

The central argument of this book is that in changing the subject matter we teach, in order to change the human subject we teach, we have come to adopt an insufficiently complex understanding of subjectivity. This oversimplification hinders our ability to make progress in cultural change. The overly simple assumptions about subjectivity that I describe derive largely from the influence of the French theorists Foucault, Lacan, Derrida, and Althusser. I will not, however, offer a critique of these theorists. I believe that their own work is much more provisional, exploratory, and useful than most of the cultural-studies applications that employ their ideas. My own theoretical paradigm, in fact, is from Lacan, whose works I have read carefully for the last twenty years. New readings of Lacan, deriving from the work of cultural theorists such as Slavoj Žižek and clinicians such as Bruce Fink and Joël Dor, have corrected many of the inaccurate representations of Lacan that circulated earlier. Krips and Stavrakakis have clarified the relation between Lacan and the social theory. Lacan's complex ideas are both readable and relevant in relation to topics currently addressed by cultural studies and composition. My goal is not to attack cultural studies but to freshen and deepen its grasp of human subjectivity, to argue for a more flexible and complex perspective that will allow cultural studies to engage students more effectively.

The primary audience for this book is scholars using cultural studies as a method for the teaching of composition. The first chapter addresses the work of James Berlin, a prominent and influential theorist whose writing helped change the subject of composition courses, making them both more theoretical and more political. The second chapter addresses the problem of desire as it affects discourse. The primary theorist for this chapter is Teresa Ebert. Ebert's "For a Red Pedagogy" makes a sharp distinction between knowledge and desire, and the sharpness of this division is something that I try to clarify and complicate by reference to Lacan's theory of the four discourses. The third chapter responds to Lester Faigley's *Postmodernity and the Subject of Composition*, which describes the challenge given to composition studies by a postmodernist subjectivity. Faigley's version of postmodernism, however, is largely represented by the work of Foucault, and it fails to take into account the role desire plays in discourse. The fourth chapter engages the work of Richard Rorty and insists that we must understand the work of discourse and composition in terms of desires and pathological attachments that need to be shifted by a dialectical process. This shift requires the work that analysts call *mourning*.[1]

Most of this book is concerned with a theory of composition, but I would hope that the claims I advance have relevance beyond composition theory. Because the subject of cultural studies unifies English departments suffering from the old literature/composition division, the kind of writing students now do in composition courses may not be terribly different from the kind of writing English majors do in upper-division courses. Therefore, I would hope the arguments I make here, primarily in relation to composition, also apply to pedagogical assumptions working in upper-division courses.

I do, however, want to give particular focus to the teaching of writing. In almost every college and university in the country, the freshman writing course is a primary rite of passage for each new student. What colleges and universities do in writing courses reflects how the academic world defines its goals and processes, and the last ten years have seen a substantial shift in these definitions. When I took a graduate course for the teaching of writing in 1976, writing was considered a skill, and grammar was considered especially helpful in the development of that skill. James Kinneavy's *A Theory of Discourse* was considered the best theoretical account of composition, and genre-defined paper assignments were routine. One need only glance at popular journals in composition (*Rhetoric Review, Journal of Advanced Composition, College Composition and Communication*) to see how things have changed.

James Berlin is a useful figure for exploring how this change progressed. Berlin's widely read theoretical essay, "Contemporary Composition: The Major Pedagogical Theories," pushed many of us to see writing from a broader and more responsible perspective than we had entertained earlier. I was just beginning my career at the time of its publication, and the essay was instrumental in persuading me to accept a position primarily in composition rather than in theory. Berlin's later essay, "Rhetoric and Ideology in the Writing Class," pushed many of us even further to see writing as part of an ideological cultural practice.

This present book takes up the discussion that Berlin began, but it seeks to connect the political aspirations of composition more thoroughly to psychological goals that I believe are important for both writing and political justice. Berlin valued the right political ideas over expressive writing. I argue that political ideas will never be right until there is attention to, and freedom in, self-expression. However, freedom is not, as most liberals assume, a simple, spontaneous act. It is, instead, a difficult discipline that requires the kind of struggle that all writers engage as they struggle to find their own conflicting thoughts and take responsibility for those thoughts on paper. My argument is heavily indebted to psychoanalytic theory, but I do not advocate that classrooms become sites for therapy. Instead, I want to describe how writing can, and should, become a mechanism for the circulation of desire within a culture.

The problem of politics is a problem of desire. It is an argument about who gets what and why. If politics is to be fair, we must fashion a culture in which everyone understands who suffers, why they suffer, and what those who suffer desire. Politics then requires a real, on-site understanding of human experience and a form of public discourse that can effectively communicate that information.

It is now a commonplace assumption in the humanities that the usual answers to arguments always come from ideological positions. I do not accept this. Complex human problems, formed by changing historical conditions, are not solved by a simple application of a correct ideology or belief structure. Instead, political issues have to respond constantly to concrete conditions of human experience, particularly experiences of suffering and enjoyment. This response is not an act of political allegiance but a fragile link to a real understanding of an actual other person in a complex context. This network of links to other people requires expressions of desire to be dispersed across a human web of communication. No group must be marginalized, and all groups must be heard as a body politic acts to solve various social problems according to some principle of an equal distribution of suffering and enjoyment.

In prior centuries, conflicts between groups of people usually took place as conflicts of what Clifford Geertz calls *primordial attachments.* In premodern societies, human attachments of blood, race, language, region, religion, and custom provided clear formulas for how people thought and acted. These attachments established social groups and set up the potential for war with other different-minded folk. Whatever passed for thinking in these groups was generally some version of a defensive justification for feelings of anger and hostility generated by the mere fact of having a primordial attachment different from that of another group.

With the Enlightenment, these primordial attachments began to break up; there was a shift in how people played out their identities. As established authorities were subjected to critique, humans had the ability to redefine themselves in relation to a polyphonic and multivalent universe of discourse. These redefinitions will always take place in an ideological context and will be responsive to ideological pressures, but it seems to me that thinking can, and should, be something other than a simple allegiance to an ideological code. It was the task of liberal thought in the past to break primordial attachments. This break has had important effects on public action and public discourse. Donald Horowitz, in *The Deadly Ethnic Riot,* argues that deadly ethnic riots have ended in America and Western Europe but not elsewhere.[2] It is difficult to explain this change as a mere effect of prosperity or democracy. America had deadly riots in the prosperous 1920s, and India, as a democratic country, continues to have race riots. The spontaneous eruption of a riot reflects a particular culture's promotion of the experience of identity.

Just as it was the task of liberal education to break attachments to primordial identities in the past, it is the task of postmodernist thought to break attachments to ideological bonds in the present. As I suggested earlier, political issues have to respond to real conditions of human experience, particularly experiences of suffering and enjoyment. It will never be possible to understand these experiences on the basis of simple ideological loyalties. Instead, we must practice a form of discourse that will allow information about suffering and desire to circulate effectively within groups of people with diverse beliefs and values. This participation in a heterogeneous discourse community requires much more than a correct ideological identity; it requires an anti-ideological identity. This identity will not be an achievement, but it can be a discipline, which in turn can be taught in writing classes.[3]

My effort to develop an anti-ideological identity differs from much of current cultural-studies practice in two ways. First, cultural studies often assumes that if we teach politically correct knowledge, we can generate politically correct practice and make political decisions to help those who suffer. I argue that the teaching of such knowledge is not enough. Such knowledge will always be used in accordance with existing ideologies and their respective desires and identities. In order to use knowledge for social progress, desire must be mobilized to use knowledge. Desire itself must be altered if knowledge is to be effective in solving social problems. Thus, I advocate a form of teaching that is responsive not simply to knowledge but also to desire.

Cultural studies most often addresses desire as if it were something that can be mobilized and corrected by the sheer demand of knowledge and/or authority. This use of authority to proscribe desire may be partly effective in the short term, but it is ultimately self-defeating in the long term. Lacan argues that desire, to an alarming extent, can be determined by a master's demand, but individuals socialized by such practice will be victimized by oppressive and charismatic leaders. It is foolish to set up English class as a place where desire is directed by some political master. As Slavoj Žižek persuasively argues, authoritarian societies are doomed to create socially isolated groups and to perpetually invent enemies to defend their exclusionary practices. They generate social relations that make social life more, rather than less, indifferent to individual suffering. They generate forms of conflict that are less, rather than more, able to reach resolution through discourse.

Using an analysis of the classic Milgram experiment, in *Obedience to Authority*, as a concrete example of my argument, I suggest that human emotions are very much determined by ideology, by loyalties to masters and ideologies. In the Milgram experiment, a victim apparently suffers, but most subjects involved in the experiment perceived that suffering as unimportant or insignificant because of their loyalties to the master. Some subjects, however, showed an ability to think independently of the master, and they sought to help the victim. Using psychoanalytic theory, I argue that all subjects had some awareness of the victim's pain, even felt anxiety in the face of it, but failed to act on their perceptions because of unconscious acts of identification that led to the repression of their feelings. The truth of the master's discourse, Lacan argues, operates by means of repression. I generalize from this example to suggest that many contemporary political problems remain as problems precisely as the result of ideological loyalties, which work as understandings that repress the real evidence of human pain.

In order to undo such repression and false understandings, it is necessary to give up identifications with the master. This act can be understood in terms of the psychoanalytic processes of identification, symptom formation, and mourning, but this does not mean that a teacher practices therapy in the classroom. Instead, the teacher simply helps students to recognize the complexity of their own emotional lives and to mourn their need for masters who offer simple explanations of complicated human phenomena. Using Jeffrey Berman's work on student writing, I argue that helping students to take responsibility for mourning is possible, and it is important to the teaching of writing.

The general scope of this book explores what Slavoj Žižek and Judith Butler term the *pathological attachments* that people form in discourse. It argues that discourse is not some neutral code able to be recoded at will. Discourse, instead, is rooted in primitive psychological functions. Changes in discourse require not simply thought but also an emotional work that requires of teachers both time and patience.

It is now commonplace for theorists to justify their support for a particular ideology as something that simply cannot be avoided in teaching. Catherine Chaput, for example, observes: "While this pedagogy might appear to impose my politics on the classroom, I believe that we are well beyond any assumption that denies the pervasiveness of politics inside and outside the classroom" (65). While it is true that politics and ideology are everywhere, this truism does not lead logically to the conclusion that we should teach a particular correct ideology. Teaching a particular ideology oversimplifies the quest for political justice and the real power dynamics behind any oppressive discourse.

Responsible political activity requires, as Chaput herself observes, "the need for criticism and self-criticism" (64). This kind of criticism requires something more than an exercise in ideological loyalty; it requires an exploration of our emotional defenses, our needs for what Lacan terms a *master,* and our inability to live comfortably with an awareness of our own limitations and ignorance.

The Enlightenment has perhaps made most of us unable to believe in any central authority, but it has not absolved us of our need for authority. Increasingly, politicians, and even academics, promise us answers to all our personal and political problems. As Aristotle observed, rather than discover the usefulness of these answers through debate, analysis, and reflection, all of us will simply choose some authority to believe. In this way, identification with a master short-circuits whatever complex action of thought is necessary for being responsive to a social dialectic that is crucial to any advance in political action.

I advance an ethics of identity that is suspicious of masters. Rather than support a theory of composition that purports to teach the correct ideology, I want to advocate a theory of democratic participation that allows information about human experience to circulate in discourse communities with the least amount of pathological distortion—that is, without the translations and libidinal coercions that all ideologies make in order to justify and maintain their own power. When understandings of other people operate as simple ideological formulas, other people are not understood. While it may be true, in a certain limited sense, that we are always in ideology, this does not mean that ideology is equal for all people in all conditions. Ideology does, as Althusser and Catherine Belsey argue, make the contradictions of social life invisible. It does create imaginary representations for our relations to material reality, but contradictions made invisible by ideology can also be made visible. This is the goal of consciousness-raising, and this activity has played an important role in race relations and gender relations in America. Psychoanalytic theory can help us, as teachers, better understand the work of consciousness-raising and better engage in the difficult task of unbinding our emotional ties, and those of our students, to ideology. If we are bound to ideology in our emotional life, the depth of our emotional life (as psychoanalytic practice shows) also provides us with evidence for undoing blind emotional attachments. As the Milgram experiment suggests, we can more fully understand the emotional experience of another person when we more fully take responsibility for the complex and often contradictory feelings we ourselves have.

This book offers, in part, a Lacanian theory of discourse, an explanation of how human social and emotional life needs and makes use of both the discourse of the master and the discourse of the university. Teaching must make use of knowledge and desire, but it must not seek to define knowledge as a pure effect of desire or control desire by the insistent demand of a master. Both desire and knowledge must circulate freely and must interact in order for social justice to make progress. The Lacanian theory of discourse that I offer may, in and of itself, be helpful for teachers of writing. It involves a systematic attempt to make sense of discourse in terms of human desire and the sometimes silent attachments of identification.

2 The Subject
in Postmodernist Theory
Discourse, Ideology, and Therapy
in the Classroom

Character structure is that part of the personality which has been modified by the external world to the greatest possible extent and which is no longer capable of further modification.
—Greg Mogenson, "The Psychotherapy of the Dead"

Nonetheless, it is necessary to learn from experience, especially when the experience is one of suffering.
—Eugene Wolfenstein, *Psychoanalytic Marxism*

Part of the influence of postmodernist theory on composition theory has been to show how ideological issues are not marginal to the role of composition instruction but central. James Berlin, in "Poststructuralism, Cultural Studies, and the Composition Classroom: Postmodern Theory in Practice," summarizes the major ideas of postmodernist theory and makes a strong argument for the importance of ideology for composition study. Berlin believes that composition instruction should provide students with a greater control and understanding of the world of discourse that surrounds and constitutes them. This control is conceived as a kind of cognitive power that students wrest from the more ubiquitous social and discursive power expressed through ideology. Ideology, as postmodernists see it, is very powerful, indeed. It works first to determine what passes as knowledge in any society and second to construct students as ideological subjects. What is meant here is not that students have ideological ideas but that subjectivity is ideological in nature. The human subject is an entity *subjected* by discourse to ideology.

I largely support the postmodernist composition goals Berlin advocates, and I agree with Berlin that "the complexities of theory have immediate pedagogical applications" (17). But because I agree with Berlin on so much, I feel it is important to argue that the human subject is more complex than Berlin and others theorize. Postmodernist theory is still in a state of evolution, and its current account of the subject is insufficiently complex for understanding relationships among language, subjectivity, and ideology.

9

Berlin's essay itself suffers from an unproductive tension between the human subject described by his postmodernist theory and the human subject appearing in his actual description of classroom practice. If Berlin had allowed his description of classroom behavior to become more fully integrated with his theoretical claims, he might have been prompted to formulate a more Lacanian description of the subject that would lead, I believe, to more useful ideas both for negotiating the ideological conflicts generated in the classroom and for achieving the cognitive power he sought. In Book II of *The Seminar,* Lacan's subject is more structured than the postmodernist subject Berlin describes, and it is structured by a libidinal signification that it cannot easily bring into responsible self-awareness in the manner Berlin describes. In the following pages, I demonstrate the contradictions in Berlin's account of the postmodernist subject's construction by ideology, and I suggest that a Lacanian model of subjectivity can help us to better understand and address the students (the real subjects) we hope to teach.

Berlin's article begins by folding older poststructuralist ideas into the more complex claims of postmodernist theory. Unlike the old poststructuralist subject, Berlin's postmodernist subject occupies no simple or stable discourse position. All of us, Berlin observes, "possess multiple selves," and for this reason, "members of an audience cannot simply activate one subject position and switch off all others" (22). Because subjectivity moves about within many and different subject positions, the responses of people to speech are complex and unpredictable. Unlike the rigidly structured poststructuralist subject, the postmodernist subject is protean and plastic, a linguistic structure of complex conflict and multiple alliance-shifting among various positions.

Berlin argues, however, that the heterogeneous plasticity of the postmodernist subject should not imply that human behavior is random or arbitrary. A person's construction through discourse is shaped by ideology, and ideology provides stability and pattern to human behavior. "Ideology," he says, "brings with it strong social and cultural enforcement, so that what we take to exist, to have value, and to be possible seems necessary, normal, and inevitable" (23). We should notice that Berlin makes two claims about ideology. First, he describes what ideology offers a culture; it confines a culture within a restricted horizon of imagination. Second, however, Berlin observes that ideology does not function simply at the level of human imagination. It is allied with various subtle and not-so-subtle policing forces.

This observation about the external enforcement of ideology is important because Berlin, like most postmodernists, argues that it is ideology—and not some putative structure *within* subjectivity—that provides stability to the subject. "Ideology" he says, "addresses or interpellates human beings. It provides the language to define the subject, other subjects, the material and social, and the relation of all of these to each other" (23). Subjectivity is by nature a structure multiple, conflicted, and unpredictable; ideology intervenes in this structure to give it pattern and definition.

Effective composition instruction, Berlin argues, will clarify and resist the policing action of ideology. "We must take as our province," he says, "the production and reception of semiotic codes broadly conceived, providing students with the heuristics to penetrate these codes and their ideological designs on our formation as the subjects of our experience" (9). Given this objective of penetrating ideological codes, however, one must ask how it is done. How are subjects, who are subjects precisely because they have been interpellated by the discourse of ideology, able to overcome ideological victimization? Put simply, how does the subject, as one ideological composition, become another ideological composition?

In Berlin's account of teaching, the students are given knowledge about their victimization, and by means of this knowledge they are able to "penetrate these codes and their ideological designs." The word *penetrate* is significant. How should we imagine this act of penetration? Is penetration a cognitive act? If it is, does this mean that Berlin's pedagogy is essentially another version of liberal humanist ideology in which freedom, rationality, and knowledge become the means for personal and social change?

A key question is, does Berlin's term *penetration* imply some new educational activity that postmodernist theory can better describe and facilitate, or does the term obscure a rigorous conceptual analysis necessary for fully understanding changes in subjectivity? *Penetration* is a loaded term; it can imply a hostile invasive act, such as a stabbing, but it also has sexual implications. Is penetration, then, not only hostile but also erotic or seductive? If Berlin has chosen his words carefully, we should ask how eros and/or hostility serve in the unmasking of ideology he advocates.

In his essay, Berlin repeatedly describes himself as operating within an environment of democratic principles. "The social-epistemic classroom," he says, "offers a lesson in democracy, intended to prepare students for critical participation in public life. It is dedicated to making schools places for individual and social empowerment" (26). Lessons in democracy imply principles of rationality, choice, and recognition of self-interest, not coercion, programming, intimidation, or seduction. Democracies assume, in principle at least, that citizens, given knowledge and the freedom to act, will act in their own best interests.

Berlin's essay suggests that freedom from ideological conscription might be developed in two ways. First, the discourse of the instructor creates a context of social and discursive freedom that is unavailable elsewhere, and this serves to undo the work of ideology. Second, the classroom encourages the study of discourse as an ideological activity. This study generates debate, but it also provides students with knowledge that enables them to construct themselves actively rather than suffer the effects of others' ideological constructions.

We should recognize that despite his initial postmodernist model, Berlin's actual classroom behavior seems to depend on very traditional liberal ideals. Freedom and knowledge are the essential powers of teaching. Berlin's term *penetration,* though hinting at more complicated psychological processes, becomes pedagogy dependent on free choice and rational speech. Clearly, there are contradictions between Berlin's earlier theoretical model and his later description of classroom practice. What has happened to Berlin's theoretical rejection of a subject "moving in complete freedom in deciding how she will live" (18)? Why does Berlin describe a constructed subject in theory but a free subject in classroom practice?

There are many ways to answer this question, but the problem surfaces with particular clarity because Berlin has sought "to present as clearly as [he knows] how some of the central features of postmodern theory" (17). In seeking simple and useful clarity, Berlin makes clearly visible the contradictions in the various modules of postmodernist theory he has spliced together to fashion a persuasive pedagogy.

Many of these contradictions have been extensively debated. In 1986, Diane Macdonell's *Theories of Discourse: An Introduction* reviewed problems in discourse theory and criticized Foucault for not adequately accounting for the possibilities of political resistance. If subjects are always an effect of the ideological power of discourse, she asks, how can subjects ever resist that power? For Foucault, there is never any remainder, never anything else *in* the material of the subject to allow, encourage, or initiate such resistance. Macdonell asks passionately *"Why should there ever be resistance? From where would resistance come, and how would it even be possible?"* (122, emphasis in original).

Unhappy with Foucault's weak attempts to theorize resistance, Macdonell labors to account for the source of resistance to ideology. First, she emphasizes a pervasive "antagonistic existence of ideologies" (40). By suggesting that the subject is always composed of antagonistic ideologies (as Berlin asserts), Macdonell implies that another ideology is always already comprising the subject, and thus the subject always has the potential to be this other ideology. The reformation of subjectivity, then, is not a matter of replacing one ideological structure with another but of giving greater strength to an ideological structure that is already present, though thwarted, in the structure of subjectivity. Second, Macdonell introduces Michel Pêcheux's concept of disidentification as a description of how resistance is initiated. Disidentification, she says, "can be brought about by political and ideological practices which work on and against what prevails" (40). Macdonell, however, is vague about how these political and ideological practices actually operate. If subjects are structures of ideological conflict, and disidentification is the key to the reformation of subjectivity, according to what principle do minority exercises in disidentification gain power over majority exercises in standard ideological identification? Do minority forms of identification gain power by simply talking more, or is there some logic of persuasion involved in effective forms of disidentification? Macdonell does not answer these questions, but she ends her book by calling for more study of "reformism in discourse" (129–30).

It is significant that in the early days of poststructuralist theory, few thinkers really worried about the subject's potential to resist ideology. For Derrida, Foucault, and Althusser, the subject was conceived as a simple linguistic illusion. Much of the rhetorical power surrounding poststructuralist descriptions of the subject derived from their claims regarding an illusory subjectivity. There was no need to describe how an illusion could occupy multiple subject positions or act as an agent because these were not ideas that poststructuralist theory wanted to entertain.

For many thinkers, the power of poststructuralist theory lay precisely in its ability to explain the subject's inability to be anything other than an ideological effect. Althusser, for example, emphasized the subject's structured resistance to political knowledge. His account of the subject, though flawed, remains remarkably powerful in its analysis of the subject's entrapment by ideology. In "Ideology and Ideological State Apparatuses," Althusser explained the lack of reason involved in political identifications. How can one understand, for example, the desire of the English worker—who labors twelve hours a day, six days of the week, in a mine; whose father has died early from lung disease; whose daily life is constantly tormented by financial scarcity; whose children are sick and in need of health care that they can not obtain—to join the army during World War I and risk his life defending the system that exploits him?

Althusser's explanation is simple. Through the workings of ideology, discourse characteristically misrepresents the real conditions of existence. Ideology, he repeats often, serves to represent "an Imaginary Relationship of Individuals to their Real Conditions of Existence" (87). Through discourse, individuals confront not war but a representation of war. Discourse functions so that what is at stake for the subject in the crisis of war is not the death of the biological human individual but the death of the ideological system that constitutes the subject. The subject, we must understand, is not the biological individual but the discourse *effect* produced by a dominant ideology whose purpose is precisely to create subjects *subjected* to the system. Subjects thus show more courage in risking biological death than they do in risking ideological death. As many insisted in America not long ago, "I would rather be dead than red." Althusser argued that subjects are not rational and free human agents able to recognize and act in their own self-interest, as we imagine through the lens of liberal humanism. Subjects are ideological constructs trapped within the ideological net of language.

For Althusser, ideology is not something external to subjectivity. Ideology is not a belief system that individuals freely have, adopt, or exchange, such as clothing or food preferences. Ideology is the condition of being an individual. Althusser insists, "there is no ideology except by the subject and for subjects. Meaning, there is no ideology except for concrete subjects, and this destination for ideology is only made possible by the subject: meaning, by the category of the subject and its functioning" (170). For Althusser, then, freedom and rationality can never be the means for ideological change, because they are not qualities innately given to subjects, as liberals assume; they are idealized concepts that the condition of subjectivity, in fact, makes impossible.

This emphasis on the passive nature of the poststructuralist subject has served as a powerful explanation of the resistance of individuals to political analysis. It appeals to clear facts about human behavior, and it fashions poststructuralist ideas in such a manner as to form a compelling political analysis, but this emphasis on the passive nature of the subject raises problems. As a theoretical description of human subjects, Althusser's account implies that individuals could never have freedom for political resistance. Paul Smith points out, in *Discerning the Subject,* that "as for Marx, the 'individual subject' for Althusser remains simply dominated" (17). Althusser's analysis of the subject thus provides an excellent account of the subject's *resistance* to ideological insight but a poor account of the subject's *capacity* for ideological change.

Smith criticized the tendency of Marxist theory to see ideology as always negative and criticized the passive nature of the poststructuralist subject:

> If ideology is seen in this way and if the subject in history is always to
> be seen as simply sub-jected to social formations, there can be no room
> for a genuine theory of resistance, or indeed, for any impulse to social
> change on the part of the subject/individual. (12)

Seeking to make resistance theoretically possible, Smith uses Lacanian theory to complicate Althusser's ideological subject. The subject Smith describes is not a unified structure of ideology but a conflicted and heterogeneous collection of ideological discourse. By giving greater attention to Lacanian subject functions (the Unconscious, the Imaginary, etc.) manipulating discourse, Smith sought to theorize greater powers of agency for the subject and to free the poststructuralist subject for political action.

Smith's discussion of the problem provides postmodernist theory with a more complex notion of the subject. Berlin refers to Smith several times in the course of his essay. Berlin's summary of this current model of the subject, however, and his description of how all this theory will work in the classroom exacerbates the problems always latent in the poststructuralist account of the subject and in Smith's account of the subject, which is most clear in its analysis of the problem of resistance but most vague in its attempt to solve it.

The effortless transformation of the poststructuralist subject from one that is a *victim* to a postmodernist subject that can be an *agent*—this easy theoretical flip from a theory that explains the subject's *incapacity* for political insight to a theory that facilitates the subject's *capacity* for political resistance—is an appeal to our own fantasies for power and success. Let us be more realistic about our profession and ourselves. Let us more carefully consider the transformations we are encouraged to put our faith in.

Smith's description of the postmodernist subject is simply a move from one limited theory of the subject to another limited theory of the subject. Smith explains what Althusser is unable to explain: the subject's potential for fluid transformation. But Smith cannot explain what Althusser explains easily: the subject's resistance to transformation. Althusser's theory, unlike Smith's and Berlin's, insists that the stability of ideology is not found in some ideological realm of discourse outside subjectivity but precisely in the structure of subjectivity itself. This sobering recognition requires more careful attention. It explains what can happen in classrooms that seek to provide students with freedom of ideological choice.

In my experience, students listening to political analysis in an English class hear two messages. First, they hear such a discourse as an articulation of a political identity. Second, they hear an explanation of human behavior, but if they disagree with this explanation, they are more energetic in thinking about why they disagree with the message than in considering the concrete examples and relationships that make up the message. Terry Eagleton, in *Ideology: An Introduction*, emphasizes Peter Dews's argument, in *Logics of Disintegration*, that while subjects are in one sense interpellated by discourse, they can also *interpret* any discourse attempting to interpellate them (145). This active, conscious response to ideological discourse is a particular feature of the subject's capacity for resistance, and it expresses the energetic workings of defensive subject functions that mediate between the discourse that characteristically represents the subject and the discourse that addresses the subject.

In some cases, student responses to oppositional political discourse can be quite extreme. They perceive such discourse not as a teacher's honest expression of identity but as an act of political terrorism. Like the subjects described by Althusser, they are assassinated as subjects by a discourse that purports to be educational. What is at stake for them in such discourse is simply survival. They would rather be dead (silent, resentful, unthinkingly hostile) than "red," and they vilify any practice that would seek to intensify such classroom warfare.

English teachers often show considerable desire to change other subjects by means of careful explanation and argumentative repetition of political beliefs. Such a desire assumes that subjects, given enough time, can be brought by means of discourse to the truth of certain discourse claims. George Orwell, in *Homage to Catalonia,* records how antifascist soldiers on the front lines in the Spanish Civil War were given not only combat duty but also what was termed *shouting-duty:*

> In every suitable position men, usually machine-gunners, were told
> off for shouting-duty and provided with megaphones. Generally they
> shouted a set-piece, full of revolutionary sentiments which explained to
> the Fascist soldiers that they were merely the hirelings of international
> capitalism, that they were fighting against their own class, etc., etc., and
> urged them to come over to our side. This was repeated over and over
> by relays of men; sometimes it continued almost the whole night. (42)

Orwell argues that this repetition had some success, but he also points out that shouting-duty operated in terms of something more than abstract political argument. Cold, dead-tired, and hungry soldiers in the fascist lines were forced to listen to claims such as: "Buttered toast . . . We're just sitting down to buttered toast over here! Lovely slices of buttered toast" (43). Certainly, even with the inducements for buttered toast, it was not the case that many soldiers (most of them unwilling conscripts) exposed to an entire night of this repetitive political explanation changed their ideas by morning and walked to the antifascist lines. Most soldiers stayed in their trenches, and though their heads were filled with antifascist ideas, their (own? inner?) thoughts were allied to fascist goals.

Human subjects, while they do show multiple and conflicting identities, also reveal defensive resistances to discourse manipulation. If you "fill" a person's mind with new discourse, there is little chance that person will *be* this new discourse. Real-world experience suggests that something apparently *within* a subject mediates between discourse that is characteristic of a particular subject and discourse that seeks to change a subject's identity. Something within a subject operates to preserve and maintain a characteristic identity. This mechanism (much of psychoanalytic theory describes it in terms of *libidinal investments* and *defensive subject functions*) prompts subjects to actively challenge rather than passively internalize the discourse they are given. Because of a kind of adhesive attachment that subjects have to certain instances of discourse, some discourse structures are characteristic of subjects and have a temporal stability. These modes of discourse serve as symptoms of subjectivity: they work repetitively and defensively to represent identity.

Subjects contain a great deal of discourse, but some modes of discourse, because they are libidinally invested, repeatedly and predictably function to constitute the subject's sense of identity. Other instances of discourse, though contained by the subject, are not libidinally invested; this language may be *in* the subject, but it simply lies dormant, having no effect whatever on subject functions.

For example, consider an analogy to the computer. The language contained by the operating system of a computer is crucial in determining how the computer behaves. The language contained within the database of a computer, on the other hand, generally has no effect on how the computer behaves. Information contained within these two different levels of computer organization functions very differently and may operate almost autonomously from each other. One field of contained language *operates* the computer. The other field is *operated on* by the computer under the directions of information contained in the previous field. If one were to enter the command *stop* into a database, the computer could display the command, but the command would have no effect on the computer. It would continue to run. If one were to enter this command into the operating system, the computer would cease to operate.

What matters in the discourse that subjects receive is not what is in the discourse, but *where* the discourse takes up residence in the organization of the subject. English teachers can teach a student to remember the ideas of Terry Eagleton, but the student may simply use these ideas as arguments to illustrate the failure of progressive education.

Humans, like computers, are organized by language, and like computers, they process language according to different principles of operation determined by basic inner components. Human subjects, like computers, constantly interact with and employ the language of the external world and are very much an effect of discourse. But this description "effect of discourse" conceals the complex mechanisms that make both humans and computers something other than simple reflectors of external discourse.

Lacanian theory suggests that subjects, in their adhesive attachment to discourse, defend and tenaciously repeat the symptoms of their subjectivity. Lacan's description of subjectivity as a form of defense should lead us to appreciate more fully the problems of penetrating or undoing the libidinal attachments subjects have to discourse. Lacan's theory of the subject, like Althusser's, suggests that subjectivity is not, as Berlin suggests, an amoeba eagerly absorbing all the discourse that it encounters. It is more like an insect with a hard exoskeleton that protects its inner structure from penetration, from the hostile invasive facts and discourse that threaten its image of contained and harmonious self-identity.

Berlin evades the question, How does the subject rebel against the ideological discourse that defensively maintains its own subjectivity? The work of Lacan and Althusser, reflecting the evidence of everyday experience, suggests that many subjects would prefer to be biologically dead than to exist as different subjects of discourse. This recognition should have sobering effects on teachers who believe that a simple, clear, and rational explanation of political activity can directly lead to different political identifications. Too often, these explanations fail to work precisely because they function not as explanations but as threats to the life principle of the subject.

Berlin's account of the postmodernist classroom labors to overcome a variety of contradictions that repeatedly subvert the theoretical rigor of his argument. Berlin claims to understand the subject's constructed nature and its *inability* to be rational and free, but he advocates a pedagogy that is absolutely dependent on the subject's *ability* to be rational and free. Berlin's account of classroom activity relies on our implicit trust in rationality to lead us effortlessly and silently to believe that as subjects penetrate the codes that produce their suffering, they will reform themselves as linguistic codes to reduce that suffering. We are also encouraged to believe that this transformation will miraculously hold its structure for a significant period of time after the student leaves the classroom and begins to operate within the larger world of a dominant ideology.

Berlin's account of a liberating postmodernist pedagogy depends on two contradictory and highly suspect models that purport to describe changes in political identity. The first model, which Berlin appeals to in his description of classroom practice, is an awkward synthesis of humanist and postmodernist beliefs. In the classroom, Berlin assumes that because the subject is a structure of ideological conflict, that particular conflict can lead naturally to a kind of resolution through knowledge and political action. This is a humanist belief that assumes that conflicts in subjectivity can find solutions by means of rational thought. This idea is loosely tied to a postmodernist assumption that subjectivity is a kind of code that can be understood and modified.

Berlin's more thorough postmodernist theoretical description of subjectivity, however, contradicts his first model's promise of a natural resolution to conflict through reflection and examination. Nothing in Berlin's version of postmodernist theory suggests any possibility for resolving the conflicts within subjectivity. The postmodernist subject, unlike the humanist subject, is *essentially* a structure of discourse conflict; it has no mechanism or motivation for being anything other than such a structure of conflict. A teacher could never hope to change the structure of, or resolve the conflict in, a subject by merely adding more discourse or more conflict to the subject. The subject would not change in structure or belief; it would simply *be* a larger and more unpredictable pool of discourse and conflict. This is true because postmodernist theory posits no mechanism that operates to select, organize, and maintain identity in relation to discourse. No mechanism within subjectivity works to construct a particular identity from the much larger collection of discourse representations and conflicts that animate it.

If the postmodernist subject can learn something about its own disorganized conflict, and then be something other than this disorganized conflict, then it is not the entity described by Berlin's postmodernist theory. Consider various metaphors for representing this transformation of the subject described by Berlin's postmodernist pedagogy but not theoretically explained by it. How does the subject, let us say, step aside for a moment from the conflict that it is and then choose for its identity a resolution to this conflict? Perhaps the subject acts in this way, but if so, the moment the subject steps aside from the conflict it is claimed to be, it reveals itself as *not* the conflict that it is claimed to be. The moment the subject shows its ability to distance itself from its own socially constructed discourse conflict, it reveals itself as something other than a mere passive effect of discourse. It is always already in potentiality another structure behind the structure it steps aside from.

Suppose the subject does not step aside from its own identity but is, in some way, presumably by language or oppositional ideology, pushed aside from its identity. This would explain how subjects are not free but are effects of ideological practice. This description would restore Althusser's account of the subject as an effect of discourse.

This idea of subjects becoming transformed through external discourse is the second model Berlin appeals to when describing the possibility for political change in the classroom. In this essentially structuralist model, change occurs not from within subjectivity but through the discourse dynamics operating in the classroom. In this model, the subject never has freedom, never chooses anything. The subject simply responds, as an automaton of discourse, to the pressure of discourse. The subject is pushed by external discourse into another structural form.

This model for political change, however, is also highly questionable. If the subject is pushed by discourse, we need to describe clearly how this pushing occurs. Is pushing an effect of the simple *exposure* of discourse to the subject, or is pushing somehow a more complicated act, an effect especially responsive to particular words, feelings, and argumentative complexity? Most scholars would agree that the push of discourse is a rather complicated linguistic, emotional, and psychological process. All examples of discourse are not equal in terms of the push they embody. Some discourses show a more powerful rhetorical push than others.

The subject does not generally represent itself as whatever language it is given. The subject is not, like a mirror, a faithful reflection of the ideological discourse external to it. The subject may be an effect of ideological codes, but it is not a *simple* effect. The subject is formed not by the simple *presence* of discourse but by a rather specific interaction of rational and irrational, emotional and repressive, forces linked to a push that is somewhere or somehow in ideological practice and engages subjectivity in *particular* and *specific* ways. To understand the push of a discourse, however, we need both more theory and more careful observation of subjective behavior. What do we mean by language if we want to say that one language structure (discourse) can push another language structure (subjectivity)?

Rather than shifting between Berlin's two inadequate models for changes in political identity, let us consider a third model for change. This model, essentially a psychoanalytic model, suggests that discourse or language is, in itself, a highly heterogeneous substance. On one hand, it can operate as coded information, able to influence political identity largely in terms of the old liberal categories of knowledge and truth. (In a later chapter, I discuss this function in terms of Lacan's discourse of the university.) On the other hand, discourse can act as a highly libidinal substance. It is the material embodiment of human emotion, emotionally charged thinking, and emotionally intense identification. This libidinal language is, in fact, the material instrument of subjective penetration: "seductive" rhetoric, invasive fantasy, and hostile assertion.

A cogent postmodernist and cultural pedagogy requires an understanding not simply of ideology but of the libidinal power of ideological language and of the power of an anti-ideological language. The libidinal power of language is found in its potential for attachments, attractions, organizations, repulsions, and bindings that create relatively stable sites of identification and disidentification wherein subjects locate themselves in a particularized language. Libidinal language refers in part to bodily experiences (often sensed as emotion) that signal the libidinal attachments that humans have to objects and ideas represented by language. To be attentive to libidinal language, we must develop a pattern of attentiveness somewhat different from the one we use in considering the meaning of ideological language.

The push of libidinal language involves a pressure and rhetorical interplay of emotion. Some of these emotions are quite apparent to us, such as aggression and erotics, but other emotions are largely unconscious, such as our happy and unquestioned identifications. Berlin provides a quick glimpse of these emotional forces in operation when he describes the classroom at times as a scene of "spirited exchange" (32), but he makes no attempt to theorize how these forces can operate in the classroom even though they may be crucial for the heuristics he wants to teach. To be clear, consistent, rational, and penetrating about the claim that subjects are pushed by language, we need a theory of libidinal pushing to complicate a theory of ideology and subjectivity.

Paul Smith insists that "to account for human agency and its actions—resisting or passive—in the face of ideology, social theory must begin to apprise itself of what psychoanalysis has to say about their shared problematic—the place of the 'subject' within structures of power and domination" (69). Psychoanalytic theory, while severely limited in its ability to describe ideological structures, must make a contribution to postmodernist theory because psychoanalytic theory has been most careful in describing the rational and irrational roles in terms of which subjectivity responds to linguistic inducements toward change. Psychoanalysis, in short, provides resources for explaining the libidinal nature of language, the libidinal construction of subjectivity, and the libidinal transformation of subjectivity.

Paul Smith's account of the subject argues that the construction of the subject is in and through language, but also that this construction is mediated by unconscious forces that complicate the overt message of any text with a copious and heterogeneous profusion of preconscious and unconscious libidinal meanings. Linguistic pressure is thus located in the structure and codings of language. It is an effective tool we all respond to and struggle to use in our daily attempts to be clear and persuasive. This libidinal force, though enormously powerful, is also irrational, often unconscious, and generally resistant to conscious intervention and control.

Berlin describes ideological conflict as if it were linguistic codes a subject could logically read and rewrite. He wants to be rational and appeal to the subject's ability to recognize conflictual codings and be free from bad conflict, even though he recognizes that the conflicts discovered in these codings can lead to heated defensive arguments and passionate emotional alliances. Berlin's essay calls for but does not develop a theory that would grasp the power of ideology in terms of language's conflictual libidinal signification.

Postmodernist theory, as Berlin describes it, implicitly suggests that political injustice is maintained by unconscious conflict. Subjects, he argues, are composed of heterogeneous organizations of discourse, but ideology imposes organization on this disorganization. I want to emphasize that we see this very abstract claim in concrete terms. In the next chapter, I will describe subjects in Stanley Milgram's experiments on obedience who act to electrocute another person and affirm that the person is not harmed, even as they respond to the victim's cries of pain with hesitation and anguish. It is clear that there are conflicted emotions and repressed feelings at work here, and it seems clear that ideology works best when it manages to keep such conflicted libidinal experiences fully repressed. Ideology, in this way, creates what Althusser terms *imaginary* relations between people.

Slavoj Žižek emphasizes the psychoanalytic dynamic of prejudice and persecution is powerfully driven by unconscious fears and poorly repressed internal conflicts. Persecution is justified by means of repression: if the social other suffers pain (because of dominant social practices), it is because this other deserves it. This explanation works because evidence that would contest such understanding cannot be entertained or brought into open service within the realm of thought.

Mark Bracher, in *Lacan, Discourse, and Social Change*, asserts: "I would go so far as to say that without reducing the unconscious conflict—whether by individual psychoanalysis, by cultural criticism, or by various other means—the chances of reducing injustice and intolerance are virtually nonexistent" (192). Reducing unconscious conflict, as analytic practice dramatically demonstrates, is not a simple matter accomplished efficiently and effectively by rational and informative speech. Saying to a person, "Look at these conflicting codes; you have unconscious conflict here," does not make that person recognize and resolve such conflict. This process of recognition (the central task of psychoanalysis but certainly not its exclusive domain) is made difficult because it is charged with all the processes of erotics, aggression, displacement, and defense (those other meanings haunting Berlin's term *penetration*) that subjects exhibit in maintaining their identities.

Many postmodernists fail to appreciate fully what is at stake in this relationship between social injustice and conflicted unconsciousness. Rhetorical scholars, especially, oversimplify the repressed tensions and desperate libidinal attachments that maintain unconscious conflict. Just as Berlin's essay labors fruitlessly to situate itself in relation to concepts such as freedom and rationality, many postmodernists fail to understand that freedom and rationality are neither givens, as liberals generally assume, nor empty categories, as poststructuralists generally assume. Freedom and rationality are developmental tasks that must be taught and learned. This teaching and learning, however, requires an awareness of information that has been traditionally described in terms of the psychoanalytic process. Subjects will develop freedom and rationality only to the extent that they are encouraged to discover, recognize, and take responsibility for the unconscious libidinal codes of desire and repression that underwrite their own subjectivity. This freedom requires work that analysts call *grief work.* Good teachers, I think, have always been able to help students with this work, but the recent fashion of cultural studies has made us insensitive to the importance of these highly subjective and emotional concerns.

Most of what is written in the preceding section, and some of what follows, is the original version of an argument that I sent to the journal *Rhetoric Review* in 1995. This material, in its very first draft, had another ending. In the earlier draft, I ended the discussion by emphasizing and giving examples of the differences between libidinal language and rational language. As my essay went through the review process, many events led me to change my original conclusion. I wrote a second version of the ending very quickly, responding to a number of strong personal feelings that developed in me as different readers of my argument responded. Because the second ending was published and seemed to support the argument effectively, I will re-present it here, even though the original version was very much tied to events that took place in 1995. Here is what I wrote in 1995:

> Rather than include my original concluding section here, however, I have decided to try to publish it later. I will end this present essay on a more personal note—(following one reviewer's suggestion) with more generalized reflections upon the issues I have raised.
>
> This article has had a somewhat unusual history in going to press. My present essay begins with the claim: "If Berlin had allowed his description of classroom behavior to become more fully integrated with his theoretical claims, he might have been prompted to formulate a more Lacanian description of the subject that would lead, I believe, to more useful ideas both for negotiating the ideological conflicts generated in the classroom and for achieving the cognitive power which

Berlin seeks." When I originally wrote this sentence it was a hypotheti-
cal claim, responding to an anonymous reader's suggestion for sharpen-
ing the focus of my argument. I accepted this suggestion as essentially
correct without worrying about much more than the ability of the sentence to reflect my understanding of Berlin's essay and my desire to
summarize the argument I wanted to develop.

What I did not know at the time was that the reviewer who
suggested this wording was in fact James Berlin himself. Berlin had
reached many of the same conclusions that I was arguing for in the
essay. Although my original draft had argued with him pointedly and
even harshly on various issues, Berlin admired the argument and
wanted it published. As a reviewer, he wrote to Theresa Enos, editor of
Rhetoric Review: "I have been reading in the very Lacanian materials
the author mentions in the essay in preparation for a book entitled *A
Teacher's Guide to Cultural Studies.* Here I had planned to include a more
detailed discussion of the subject in the postmodern epistemic rhetoric
class."[1]

Berlin had hoped, when this essay was published, to respond with a
short reply. "Should my essay be published along side hers?" he wrote
to Enos. (Berlin had read my sex incorrectly.) "When do you need my
response? (Since I feel a lot is at stake here, I can safely promise that I
will be right on time with my essay." Berlin, however, could not be on
time with his response. He died about a month after he wrote his letter
to Enos, and his reply to this essay will not be forthcoming.

And yet, because of Berlin's extended letter, I can quote some of his
reactions. Berlin was uneasy with the emphasis that I was giving to personal experience: "I want to keep a good discussion on track, one that
this author goes a long way toward starting. I also want to address some
small disagreements, such as the distinction made between the central
place of ideology in abstract politics and the lack of ideology in the
libidinal attachments of the subject. This separation does not hold up
to analysis, as Kaja Silverman and other feminists have shown. This dis-
agreement is important since the wrong take on it can lead the expressivists in the audience to once again abandon the political and public in
favor of the libidinal and private. This has already appeared in certain
commentators on poststructualist theory who call upon the challenge
to foundations and the split subject to argue for a revival of Peter Elbow
and the celebration of the personal."

I am uneasy with Berlin's refusal to see differences between ideological structure and libidinal structure. I do, however, now see the need to
approach these issues with care.

In my earlier draft I had argued that political thinking typically
reflects the surface manifestations of a variety of values that are
held most tenaciously at an unconscious libidinal level. Thus logical

argumentation of the sort that Berlin wants to develop in the classroom typically does not address the real binding effects of ideology. Too often, logical and informative arguments have no effect on the commitments students have to ideology. This is true because the *real* binding effects between subjectivity and discourse are not made in relation to linguistic representations but in relation to structural patterns of identity that are mapped out libidinally in the body. The body operates as the deep structure for much of language, the space where adhesive attachments to discourse are made.

I had originally wanted to emphasize that ideological structure can be separate from libidinal structure. Libidinal attachments, I argued, are not mental attachments to ideas that can be adopted or dismissed by logical reasoning but bodily attachments that must be explored in a language other than the language of politics or utopian thought. These networks of libidinal attachments *prestructure* in advance any thinking a subject might do on a particular subject.

Berlin and others have helped me to see that libidinal structure *is* always ideological. Libidinal structures are inescapably ideological because all meanings and all feelings operate as meanings in an ideological context. While this is true, it should not, however, imply that ideology and libidinal structure are essentially the same mechanism. It is not the case, for example, that all conscious thought is equally ideological and libidinal. Let me use a concrete example to develop this point.

When I was a Peace Corps volunteer in India one of my in-country language teachers became physically sick to her stomach when she discovered I was eating cow. When she first told me she thought that she would be sick because of what I was eating, I laughed. Both she and I were rational tolerant people, but we discovered a subject in relation to which we could express how we felt, but we could not easily change what we felt. Let us consider what is present to subjectivity—present to subjectivity beyond the dimension of rational thought—in her "funny" sickness and my "sick" laughter.

Both her sickness and my laughter is a bodily response of subjectivity to an ideological value. This response is performed for us, in advance, before either of us have a chance to think or reason. She sees meat and is sick. I see her response and find it funny. These responses have been set in place by ideological values that work upon our bodies before we begin to think. And to the extent that neither of us can separate ourselves from these bodily responses, we can't really change our values even if we do manage to talk rationally about the value of eating cow meat. We can discuss food habits and state our preferences, but the discourse work necessary to *call into question* in a realistic manner the value of eating cow meat requires more than simple talk; it requires changes in bodily experience—transformations in libidinal attachments.

It requires an ability to distance ourselves from our own gut-level values in order to more comprehensively judge these values.

This example and other similar examples suggest to me that Freud's theory of libidinal organization needs to be more carefully examined. Libidinal networks, he argues, exist as another system of meaning operating in relation to but also independent of our conscious use of language. In my example this bodily libidinal attachment speaks in terms of food values, but it can just as easily speak powerfully in terms of any ideological value. Thus any subject "properly" trained in ideological values is likely to say not simply that cow meat makes me sick, but hippies make me sick, or blacks make me sick (racism), or homosexuals make me sick (homophobia), or poor people make me sick (Republicans?). And anyone from another perspective is likely, before he or she thinks, to either laugh or become enraged by this statement.

The preceding material is what I wrote and published in 1995, and these paragraphs seemed to strike a nerve for many readers. First, and most important, Berlin's death was still a painful memory. The quotation from Berlin spoke with a poignancy that I could never have attained in my own voice. Second, my own attempt to make sense of my argument by means of my own Peace Corps experience was a much more effective illustration and development of my claim, much better than the very rational, abstract, and theoretical claims I made in the earlier draft. I now believe that these events added evidential weight to my argument. We are moved by emotion—by libidinal attachment and loss of libidinal attachment—much more than by our rational arguments. What we *are* in discourse is not evenly spread across all examples of discourse. We are *in* those discourse clusters that bind our emotion, and this binding of subjectivity to discourse is something we need to better understand.

The remainder of this book will seek to develop this better understanding. My central argument is that the rhetoric of discourse is libidinal. Some examples of discourse are libidinal for us; they elicit our strong response, attention, and interest. Other examples of discourse are inert representations that we handle like packages. (As I explain later, Lacan calls this the *discourse of the university.*) We can move them about in various places in our mind, but they really have no effect on our feelings, thoughts, beliefs, or motives.

Freud argues that our libidinal attachments and detachments are not something that we can easily control through rational and abstract thought. This fact is seen with special poignancy in the case of mourning. In "Mourning and Melancholia," Freud points out that while we may know that a person we love is dead, we cannot simply abandon our libidinal attachments.

We may logically know that who we love exists no more, and we may recognize that we must, in many senses of the words, *give up* what we have lost. We must abandon and transform libidinal attachments. But contrary to our conscious decisions, our attachments persist in terms of memory, desire, image, and emotion. Mourning shows the extent to which we will all insist on having that which we cannot have, even when we know that our desire for an object is futile, irrational, or impossible.

The work of giving up a libidinal attachment is not a rational act of thought but a painful and protracted mode of reflection. The giving up of libidinal attachments is always a form of mourning; it is a complicated labor we perform on the many and varied imagery of that to which we are attached. The work of mourning is always initially rejected, but later this work becomes both isolating and deeply absorbing. This work is especially difficult, Freud says, because we must painfully withdraw our attachments from each and every memory image that still unconsciously maintains and insists on maintaining our libidinal attachments. The person mourning is like a youth who has lost a lover yet remains attached, seeing and feeling a deeply haunting image everywhere.

If libidinal attachments show great durability (as the work of mourning indicates), they also show highly intense fixations on *particular* objects. Using a story from well-known analyst Harry Guntrip, Robert Rogers suggests that humans fundamentally seek neither pleasure nor sex but specific forms of attachment.

> Fairbairn poses to a child whose mother has cruelly thrashed her:
> "Would you like me to find you a new, kind Mummy?" The child answers, "No I want my own Mummy" (Guntrip 1975, 146). In the context of attachment theory, one can say that the strength of the child's tie to a particular mother—however harsh she may be—infinitely outweighs the possible desirability of any substitute figure. . . . In the presence of anxiety or difficulty (being thrashed) the child paradoxically needs the attacking object more than ever. (25)

John Bowlby's groundbreaking work on attachment shows clearly that children who are forced to live without their mothers consistently show modified behavior—almost always hostile or depressive behavior. Curiously, attachment behavior reveals itself as an inflexible need for specific objects; substitutes are not accepted.

The specificity involved in attachment helps explain why humans are resistant to change and are not as resilient and plastic in ideological change as many postmodernist descriptions imply. While the early Freud wanted to describe the human subject as a pleasure-seeking organism, the later

Freud saw that humans were often strangely attached to behavior that led inevitably and repeatedly not to pleasure but to pain. Some particular attachments, formed by a variety of factors, are not given up, even when they cause considerable pain. We expect an organism experiencing pain to move away from the object causing the pain, but in many cases, this is not a realistic expectation.[2]

These irrational attachments are at the center of the psychoanalytic processes that attempts to make such attachments fully conscious and to give the subject a choice to continue or not with such behavior. To the extent that analysis can make all forms of pain conscious, a subject *can* choose a pattern of identity that promises to produce the least pain. It is to this possibility for knowledge and choice, and to this possibility for the representation of pain, that reason must make its appeal. When conflicted libidinal structures repress conflicted forms of suffering, choice is not possible—subjects not only repeat habitual forms of suffering but they also typically deny that they suffer.

Political attachments are not often as strong as attachments to parents and lovers. Nonetheless, political identities reflect libidinal attachments. To understand ideology and its role in defining subjectivity, we must better understand the nature of libidinal attachment. Often, for example, it can be counterproductive to seek to change political identity by simply talking more clearly about politics. For many subjects, a discussion of politics, in the common sense of the word, can be largely diversionary from the complex and adventitious patterns of discourse interaction that need to occur for the subject to divest itself of that knotted complex of conflicted libidinal organizations, which in each concrete case define the subject and the political attachments of the community.

If ideologies are bad, they are bad not because some authority says so, but because they make us, or people we care for, suffer. This precisely is the problem. Subjects would often rather suffer from a bad ideology than suffer from changing their ideology. Ideology can the bad mother who is better than no mother.

How can teachers work with this situation, this inability of subjects to be rational about libidinal attachments? I think that the first thing we must do about this issue is understand it. If we can teach that rational judgments about conflicting libidinal attachments are painful, elusive, but immensely important, then we will perhaps be in a better position to achieve some of the political goals that Berlin advocates. This teaching will be political, but it will also be personal. Because ideology operates at the level of personal and emotional experience, it needs to be explored at that level. This dimension of the personal may not resemble the kind of personal exploration advocated by Elbow and other expressivists. It is particularly concerned with moral, political, and conflictual emotional issues, as Berlin himself advocated, but it does not emphasize liberation in terms of forming a collective identity, as idealized by Ira Shor and other social progressives. Recognition of a collective political identity is important and crucial for political action, but before we can *act* the values of a new political identity, we must first *adopt* a new political identity. This change is not easy. Deep changes in our *awareness of* and *choices for* suffering—the kind of awareness often required for the formulation of a new political identity—require mourning, and mourning is an isolating experience. It requires a space for personal reflection. No one else can do the work of mourning for us. It is not some kind of information that we can memorize and employ. Our most common response to those who try to push us toward mourning is anger and hatred, the gestures of the countertransference. Yet this change we resist may be what we most need.

3 On Unfree Speech
and the Pedagogy of Demand

In the previous chapter, I examined how James Berlin's desire for a truly democratic politics conflicts with his theory of postmodernist subjectivity. To his credit, I think, Berlin wanted to encourage free debate in his classroom, but his encouragement of free debate, as I suggested, may not lead to the kind of changes that he sought. Increasingly, there seems to be a recognition that the new liberation model of pedagogy does not lead effortlessly to happily liberated students. Richard Boyd writes:

> It was to be expected that the old narratives of instructor and student locked in a struggle of will would be replaced by a new version of a far more peaceable classroom where teachers might act more as collaborators than as adversaries. (590)

But as Boyd argues, and as Ohmann and others agree, such visions of happy students seeking self-understanding were overoptimistic. Students seem "not wanting to participate in their own liberation" (591).

This discovery of the tenacity of student resistance has generated significant scholarly response.[1] If teachers wish primarily to pursue political change, student resistance often requires a choice between democratic and authoritarian styles of teaching, both of which tend to make teachers uncomfortable. Insisting that students show preferences for "correct" political beliefs threatens democratic processes. On the other hand, if teachers make no attempt to impose their political beliefs on students, they risk being charged with cowardice in their avowed desire to make the world better.

Much has been written about the ethics of politically correct teaching. In this chapter, I review how the concept of freedom has been redefined by poststructuralist thought and how the revision of the term seems to be generating a new ethics for teaching. In the field of English studies, Stanley Fish represents the attitude of many in the title of his article, "There Is No Such Thing as Free Speech and It's a Good Thing Too." Certainly, over the last twenty years, the liberal ideal of free speech has received well-considered criticism. It is common now for universities to ban representatives of socially dangerous societies and to restrict hate speech. Law journals now publish articles that explore the fine line between free speech necessary for healthy public debate and free speech that incites violence and prejudice.

In keeping with this contemporary perspective on free speech, new theories of pedagogy have begun to advocate restrictions on students' desire to respond freely and critically to the truth claims made by teachers. Defenders of this more significant restriction on speech find support in a coherent social-constructionist theory of speech and subjectivity. This theory argues that the very ideal of free speech is a liberal illusion.

From this perspective, speech is never free; it is always conditioned. Free speech is not, as we might imagine, a choice we make when we speak; it is a discursive act determined by machinelike mechanisms that operate subjectivity. Speech may express desire, but this desire is a socially constructed entity that operates our subjectivity without our ever choosing or thinking.

Social-constructionist theory describes free speech as an effect of socially constructed desires that turn dependably, like machine cogs, in discourse production. As the cog of subjectivity turns, desires are indeed expressed. These desires are not evidence of any freedom in the acts of thinking, speaking, or desiring; they are determined by external social practices. Thus, speech is determined in advance of a thinking subject. The long-cherished ideal of free speech is not central to a healthy subjectivity; it is a simple dumb and determined mechanism and is very literally a symptom—a blind, unthinking form of repetition—of cultural practice.

This analysis of free speech leads to clear conclusions. If desire is the simple product of a cultural practice, then politically progressive teachers should not encourage freely expressed desires. They should, instead, seek to change desire. Good teaching should make desire work for the social good.

Teresa Ebert, in *Ludic Feminism and After* and her 1996 *College English* essay "For a Red Pedagogy: Feminism, Desire, and Need," argues that the free expression of desire has harmful effects. Liberty, in truth, contributes to social oppression. "Liberty is acquired at the expense of the poverty of others," she says in "For a Red Pedagogy" (813). Ebert's analysis builds on the initial claim that desire is not really free to develop a second logical consequence. When this desire that is not free leads to regrettable social consequences, it should be remedied by the application of knowledge. Given this analysis, the suppression of free speech is not a negative action but a positive, healthy, and necessary one.

Maxine Hairston documents the repudiation of free speech by the cultural left in her well-known essay, "Diversity, Ideology, and Teaching Writing."[2] Hairston's defense of free speech has been widely cited, but for many, it suffers from a lack of theoretical ground. Her argument appeals to feeling, and it is precisely feeling that social-constructionist theory has shown to be a cultural fabrication. If politically progressive teachers sometimes hurt their students, this hurt is not a bad thing if it is productive of a society, in the long run, that will create less hurt for the disadvantaged.

Some theoretical support for free speech comes from psychoanalytic scholars. Mark Bracher, for example, in *The Writing Cure: Psychoanalysis, Composition, and the Aims of Education,* argues that unconsciously determined desire, as it is expressed in prejudice and projection, is an important cause, if not the essential cause, of social injustice. Bracher's position, like Ebert's, sees experience, desire, and ideology as mechanisms of subjectivity. Rather than seeking to change desire through some discipline imposed on speech, Bracher argues that changes in desire can come about only through the free expression of desire. All changes in desire, he argues, must function like changes of desire in therapy: they can come about only through the encouragement of free speech and the recognition and integration of the unconscious desire it reveals. For the most part, however, the debate over free speech in teaching has been difficult to evaluate. Different parties to the debate speak mutually exclusive languages that place them from the outset in opposing ideological camps.

I will first represent the claims of free speech from three theoretical perspectives: humanist, social-constructionist, and psychoanalytic. After presenting each of these views as fairly as I can, I will integrate them from the broader theoretical perspective offered by Lacanian social theory. In conclusion, I will defend free speech, but I will do so in terms of a social-constructionist redefinition of why it is important for speech to be both free and socially constructed. Indeed, what I seek is desire determined by the free circulation of desire within a body politic.

The Humanist Perspective

Most defenders of free speech speak from an essentially humanist perspective. From this view, the world of discourse is a free space in which all individualized subjects participate equally by the simple verbal expression of their thoughts and feelings. Desire is something intrinsic to each individual subject and is directly expressed by each subject. In this way, desire participates freely and usefully in public discourse, which is simply the social aggregate of each person's expressed desire. Individual expressions, in principle, have the ability to circulate equally in social space, and each expression is responsive to social debate. In this expression, circulation, and responsive elaboration, individualized expressions of desire give rise to beneficial political and cultural effects.

From a humanist perspective, good health in the social sphere requires that each individual speak unique desires. This is a central principle of democracy. Individuals have the right and obligation to say what they think. Individual desire thus becomes an almost sacred element in the constitution of a social body. It is the ground that legitimates social action and directs the path of social progress through free expression.

Oddly enough, the work of Bakhtin offers a particularly useful illustration of how this dialogue of desire operates. Bakhtin is interesting to consider because (despite the contrasting accounts of language published under the name Volosinov) he has helped define a contemporary humanist attitude toward desire and free expression. While Bakhtin insists that at least half the words we speak and most of the thoughts we think come from others, some of his most influential work argues that what a person does with the words of others is always influenced by a particular individual's own unique intention.

When we speak, Bakhtin argues, we *develop* ourselves and our intentions as we adopt public discourse. Writers and speakers necessarily adopt the words of others and a public system of meaning; however, this adoption is not an absolute subjection to the meanings of public discourse. Writers and speakers inflect public language with their own particular desires. In *The Dialogic Imagination,* Bakhtin argues that the writer "does not meld completely" with the language used. Instead, the words of others as used by the writer, are "accented" in particular ways: "The prose writer makes use of words that are already populated with the social intentions of others and compels them to serve his own new intentions, to serve a second master" (300). This appropriation of language by the writer and the appropriation of the writer by language is part of what Bakhtin terms the "individual's ideological becoming" (342).

This account of intention, making use of public meaning but inflecting it in particular ways, echoes traditional humanistic perspectives on desire. Desire here is apparently the true ground of each individual's relation to all external forces, power, truth, and language. Desire, thus, is the fulcrum at which each particular subject applies pressure to social influence.[3]

The Social-Constructionist Perspective

Many practitioners of cultural studies view desire very differently from Bakhtin and the humanists. Desire is not the ground of an individual's relation to the truth and power, and it is certainly not the fulcrum for resistance to external regimes of power. Desire is not a source or a ground of anything; it is quite simply a preexisting social product. It is an energy originating outside the subject and then entering it from some external political realm. Desire may drive subjectivity, but it does not originate in subjectivity. It is the ghosting effect of the social realm that constructs subjectivity. Desire is clearly ideological, and it is most often bad ideology.

These different assumptions about desire lead to different teaching practices. When humanist teachers speak to students, they speak to some free desire that animates them. When practitioners of cultural studies speak to students, they speak to some underdeveloped principle of social justice within them that might discipline the alien desire that inhabits them. We might describe humanist forms of pedagogy as dialogical and culturalist forms as diacritical. Dialogics seeks to speak to desire and draw it out; diacritics seeks to discipline it.

For many practitioners of cultural criticism, dialogic teaching is politically suspect because it does not recognize that free desire characteristically serves the dominant social order. In leaving desire uncritically free, dialogics fails to confront those cultural symptoms that structure an oppressive society precisely though the practices of subjects who, as Althusser argues in "Ideology and Ideological State Apparatuses," "work on their own" and "freely choose" to express their desires. Thereby, in fact, those subjects repeat the oppressive social codes that have constructed them as subjects (182).

Dialogics, to the extent that it legitimates the students' need to express their desire freely, simply legitimates the dominant desires of a dominant culture. Following Marx's observation that pleasure is determined by culture, a number of cultural-studies theorists advocate a pedagogy that critiques pleasure and thus redistributes the power imbalances supported by free expression. Anthony Easthope, in "The Subject of Literary and the Subject of Cultural Studies," suggests that an important dynamic of cultural studies is to make the relation between pleasure and subjectivity problematic. If fabricated pleasures support power, then one might unravel the noose of power by unbinding the subject's subjection to pleasure. We might, Easthope says, submit "pleasure to theoretical critique" (43). If desire is (according to the dominant paradigms of cultural studies) the simple product of a cultural discipline, then social progress depends not on the expression of desire but on the critique of it.

Ebert's "For a Red Pedagogy," is particularly critical of those theoretical systems (feminist, postmodernist, and psychoanalytic) that have posited the "desiring subject as the center of its politics and its way of making sense of reality" (796). This privileging of the individual's desire, Ebert argues, leads to significant problems. In democracies, individuals do make choices on matters of policy in terms of their free expression of desire. American citizens are frequently asked to choose between paying more taxes for better schools or keeping their money to pursue their own particular pleasures. The consequences of these choices are frequently disheartening.

As Americans "think" and express their desires, other people become instances of obstruction to personal pleasure. Rather than make small sacrifices for the real material needs of others, Americans often choose to keep their surplus money and satisfy their individual desires. They choose not to pay taxes for school lunch programs for the poor; they choose not to support clinics that treat the homeless and the impoverished. There develops, in American society, an insidious equality of desires. If all desires are equal, then my desire for a new luxury vehicle is equal to your desire for food. Thus, the few who need food are denied it by a political process that allows the many to buy luxury vehicles. This injustice takes place because desire is not something simply given to individuals, but it is produced in individuals by capitalistic practices. People do not naturally want to buy luxury vehicles; they are made to desire them by social practices. These practices, it is hoped, can be changed by effective teaching.

Much of cultural studies has as its aim the criticism of culture. This usually also entails a criticism of those structures of desire that shape culture. The prevailing assumption is that criticism and knowledge can change these structures of desire that hold culture in place.

Ebert suggests that the social injustices of democracies can be corrected by a direct and forceful application of knowledge. Specifically, she argues, we must understand the difference between desire and need. It is easy to distinguish, she says, between real material needs, such as the need for food, and more superficial desires fueled by capitalist society, such as the desire for luxury vehicles. This distinction between need and desire is obvious, Ebert argues, and it should be taught. This teaching would help students sacrifice their desires as they respond to the needs of others.

Ebert's distinction between need and desire is a useful contribution to social theory, but its application raises difficult questions regarding the relations between desire and knowledge. If the distinction between need and desire is taught as a simple truth, how should teachers respond to students who get the facts wrong when they incorrectly express their desires as needs? How will Ebert respond to an incorrect articulation of desire when students express their right to buy a new luxury vehicle or vote against tax increases intended to help the poor?

Ebert's "For a Red Pedagogy" empowers teachers to correct students who get the facts wrong. The materialist critique that Ebert promotes is, she says, a "knowledge practice" (816). It is "a mode of social knowing that inquires into . . . concealed operations of economic and political power" (810). This inquiry reveals social power as something that determines the "representations" we have of our lives (810). But in describing pedagogy as a mode of understanding representations, Ebert's pedagogy, in fact, confronts students as desiring subjects and seeks to change their desire. The students must understand, Ebert suggests, that their desire is not their own, that it is alien and harmful. Further, Ebert asks that this desire be sacrificed by something called *knowledge.*

At this point, at the interface between the student's desire and the teacher's desire, the interface between the teacher's knowledge and the student's knowledge, we should seek to carefully examine how desire works in pedagogy. Ebert argues that the student's subjectivity can be, and should be, changed by knowledge; it is not at all clear, however, that knowledge as a practice has the power to make changes in a desiring subject.

The Psychoanalytic Perspective

The social justice that Ebert requires depends not simply on the truth of her distinction between need and desire but also on students' recognition of that truth. If students accept the knowledge offered by the teacher, then we would seem to have no problem, but what if students insist on their own views and mechanically and blindly, or symptomatically, reject the adjustment sought by the teacher? At this point, we need to think carefully about those coglike mechanisms that operate subjectivity.

A psychoanalytic understanding of symptoms can help here. Psychoanalytic practice demonstrates that knowledge does not easily change the symptoms expressed by people in therapy. And, in fact, one does not need to know anything about psychoanalysis to see how some individuals fixated on certain belief structures deny any and all rational evidence that contradicts their beliefs. In the larger scope of things, perhaps, it may be simply true that strong expressions of desire are seldom easily changed by simple knowledge.

We normally accept that people say, insist on, and even believe many things simply because they want to. I remember once in Iowa, when my son was three, he demanded a Coke during a blizzard. When I told him that we had no soda in the house, and it was impossible to go to the store because of the storm, he replied: "But I *want* Coke." It is not at all clear to me that adults act much differently from children in this respect.

As teachers, we commonly resist the idea that many beliefs have the literal structure of symptoms; yet it should be obvious that this is the case. In teaching, we encounter two rather different kinds of mental acts that support knowledge. We encounter both rational truth claims and symptomatic beliefs. A symptomatic belief is not the same thing as a verbal truth claim, which responds effortlessly to the pressure of demonstration and logical argument.

Consider the example of a person who chooses, because of a phobia of being eaten by sharks, to avoid public swimming pools. Imagine telling this person that there is really nothing to fear in the pool. It may be obviously true that there are no sharks hiding in public swimming pools; nonetheless, phobic swimmers may imagine these animals present. A symptomatic belief is not banished easily by what we consider proof. A person with a symptom can believe that there are sharks in a public pool and can feel compelled to act on their beliefs, even though that person also knows, in some sense, that there are no sharks in the pool.

I once had a student who wrote about her fear that she would be eaten by sharks if she stepped on the wooden floor of her bedroom. She had gone to see the movie *Jaws*, and after she came home she developed an unbearable fear of her bedroom floor. She knew, of course, that there were no sharks hidden in the wood of her floor. Even though she knew this to be true, she still feared that sharks might eat her. She told this story in my classroom, and when she tried to explain what happened, some students laughed, but she herself was very tense and serious. She described how she had moved her bed as close to the door of her room as possible and had filled her floor with her stuffed animals. She still could not move from the bed to the door without walking over some floor, and this move terrified her. In time, her parents took her to a therapist and her fear slowly disappeared.

This story indicates complex relations existing between knowledge and irrational fears or desires. Truth claims, no matter how true, no matter how well supported by established facts, do not change symptomatic behavior. Thus if a student claims, "I am against paying taxes to feed the poor," we might imagine this position to be something like a symptomatic expression. No amount of proof that the poor do not easily find work will change this student's mind. What is at stake in this belief is not a judgment about facts but irrational fears and desires that resolve themselves in a compromise formation that analysts call *symptoms*. The symptom is an expression of desire that supports a knowledge in a tenaciously nondialectical manner. The student "knows" that all people in America can be successful, but this knowledge is supported not by evidence but by simple desire.

Symptomatic beliefs supported by desires are a network of libidinal effects holding in place particular relations of language. In analysis, these affects and their related networks must be talked through various nodes of resistance in a lengthy series of staged denials, defenses, and protests. One cannot, as Ebert implies, simply insist on a factual property of reality to change a desire. Desires that are present as symptoms are primitive and resistant to alteration through discourse. Victor Vitanza, in "'The Waste-land Grows'; Or, What Is 'Cultural Studies for Composition' and Why Must We Always Speak Good of It?: ParaResponse to Julie Drew," has recently challenged classroom teachers to study the effects of cultural studies on their students. The primary questions in such a study would have to be, Vitanza observes:

> Do the students ever stop thinking and practicing racism, sexism,
> classism, age-ism; do they ever stop thinking and practicing their homo-
> phobia and self-hatred, etc.; or do they, in taking on an understanding
> of false consciousness . . . only become more cynical in their acts of
> violence against other human beings and themselves? (700)

When attacks on a bad idea do not change the idea, they strengthen the forms of defense against such attacks. I believe Vitanza correctly suggests that such defenses commonly develop as forms of cynical thinking.

The changing of the symptom in analysis typically generates signifi-cant emotional affect. Often in this talking cure, changes begin through what is termed the *transference effect of love,* but generally these changes also involve significant and diverse emotional turbulence. There is resent-ment, aggression, and not infrequently, murderous rage. Teachers seeking to change the desires of their students should expect precisely these re-sponses from their students. Many teachers of cultural studies seeking to change the desires of their students encounter these responses daily.

Rational truth claims can be changed by knowledge but symptomatic beliefs cannot. The fulcrum for any change in symptomatic beliefs is not knowledge but desire. This aspect of the relationships between desire and knowledge opens up a complex set of issues and questions that confront any teacher who seeks to change desire. These issues merit serious atten-tion, but I would like to defer them to the next chapter.

The Lacanian Perspective

If the cultural studies approach to culture suggests that desire should be changed by knowledge, the psychoanalytic response would seem to be that symptomatic desire is not changed by knowledge but hardened into an even more defensive reaction formation. If this is true, and there is much evidence to support it, this would seem to throw the issue back into the original humanist position. Teaching, if it is to change culture through desire, must rely on a dialogue that engages, expresses, and draws into motion the play of human desire.

I will not, however, end this discussion with a simple reversion to a reinstatement of the humanist position. I want to develop, in some complexity, a Lacanian reading of this issue. The Lacanian analysis is useful because it suggests, from a psychoanalytic perspective, that an authoritative insistence on knowledge can change desire. It might thus seem to support rather than deny the cultural-studies response to desire and culture. I argue, however, that changing human desire by means of an uncompromising insistence on knowledge, while it may change what many students believe, is not the solution to the problem of politics.

If we begin with even ordinary language, we might imagine that when a teacher insists on a certain truth, the teacher's relation to the student pivots on a response to demand. Lacanian theory describes how this demand becomes the ground not simply for the transmission of truth but also for the generation of a complex set of libidinal (and I emphasize here, symptomatic) relations that bind two individuals in social space. Behind the teacher's apparently humble insistence on simple objective truth, we often find a hidden erotics operating in the pressure of demand. Demand here refers not to a simple verbal command, such as "Pass the salt," but to an absolute and uncompromising expression of desire structured as demand. This demand of the teacher addresses the student in social space.

Consider what is at stake when one person makes a demand on another person. Consider the cliché of the religious right, "Accept Christ as Your Savior or Perish." In principle, any person is always free to reject someone's demand, just as anyone is, in principle, free to reject what Althusser describes as the *hail* of ideology. In reality, though, demands and ideological hails are usually successful. The reason they are successful is complicated; we might say that the person who accepts a demand wants to be recognized or please the person who makes the demand. It is in terms of this want-to-please attitude or its corollary, a fear to displease (or what Lacan formulates as a primitive need for recognition and love), that demand is successful.

Demand, Lacan argues, binds both parties to a particular set of libidinal relationships and expectations. Jonathan Scott Lee explains the Lacanian concept of demand by calling attention to children's early responses to the caregiver. Lee argues, "the child's demand for food actually masks a deeper longing for recognition by the other, recognition that will in some way make up for the child's fundamental want-of-being" (59). In demand, children ask literally for food, but what they want is something much more that is not easy to name. It is really a magic content, some impossible object that will fill in for the child's fundamental want-of-being. Often, this magic content is termed *love*, but when love is present in demand, it is generally hidden. It is a kind of absolute request that is present yet invisible in the relationship.

Dylan Evans points out that demands respond to two objects, one real and the other imaginary:

> Demand too acquires a double function: in addition to articulating a need, it also becomes a demand for love. And just as the symbolic function of the object as a proof of love overshadows its real function . . . so too the symbolic dimension of demand (as a demand for love) eclipses its real function. . . . (35)

Evans argues that under the pressure of demand a real object, such as food, acquires a second, purely symbolic function. Physically, children need the real object "milk" to live, but children as symbolic subjects also need a symbolic avowal of love. When children demand milk, they ask for a real object, milk, but they are also, in demand, asking for a symbolic object, love. When milk is given it is more than a physical object; it becomes a symbolic one, proof of love.

Demand thus plays a role in a signifying economy whenever real objects operate as symbolic proofs of love. Consider what is demanded when a teacher makes a demand on a student's free will. Why would a student comply with a teacher's demand? What exactly is involved in seeking to please a teacher's demand?

Teachers may represent their role as people who simply disseminate a simple object: the truth. If teachers address their truth to the desire of the student and judge any willful opposition to their truth with feelings of reproach, however, they present the student not simply with a literal object, truth, but with a symbolic object masking a demand. Teachers, in effect, say, "If you love me, you will believe," or, "If you want my love, you will believe." Students who want recognition or love more than the assertion of their own desire will believe not on the basis of knowledge but on the need for recognition.

In the classroom, this relationship is complicated. Sometimes there is an implication from the teacher, "If you wish to avoid my hatred, you will believe." Usually, there is a mixture of different feelings, conflicting beliefs, and ambivalent hopes. Often though, there operates a certain dialectic of intensity that oversimplifies this emotional complexity. Love is, as they say, a condition in which "You are all for me," and "I am all for you." In this case, the teacher's truth becomes all for the student, and the student's recognition becomes all for the teacher.[4]

This analysis suggests that we may find a very subjective and emphatically libidinal lure precisely where it would seem least likely, in an objective, no-nonsense style of teaching that, we might say, makes effective use of demand.

Obedience and an Example of Demand

In Stanley Milgram's classic experiments on obedience, average people are told by an authority figure to administer an electrical shock to another person, a learner. The experiment works neatly in the context of my argument because Milgram calls the learner the victim. For many years, Milgram's account of his experiment was widely read in many disciplines. The victim's task is to remember proper responses to verbal cues. The person chosen as the subject of the experiment must administer a shock whenever the victim makes a mistake. The authority figure, whom I term a teacher, and the victim are actually both actors, and the experiment is designed to discover if the experimental subject (whom I term a *student*) will deliver a lethal dose of electricity purely on request. Milgram's experiment shows that when the teacher demands the delivery of a lethal dose, the student usually complies. This, of course, was an unsettling discovery. It was, and still is, troubling to think that the average person would kill a stranger simply because a teacher demanded it.

Milgram made sense of his experiment in terms of the considerable power of what he termed *obedience*. In his book-length account of the experiment, Milgram used a "cybernetic viewpoint" to define obedience as a socially determined form of behavior that he called an *agentic state*. Milgram explains:

> I shall term this the agentic state, by which I mean the condition a person is in when he sees himself as an agent for carrying out another person's wishes. This term will be used in opposition to that of autonomy— that is, when a person sees himself as acting on his own. (133)

Milgram explained the agentic state as a "master attitude from which observed behavior flows" (133) and suggested that this state was both cybernetic and phenomenological.

When Milgram describes his obedient subjects as shifting from what he calls a *state of autonomy* to an agentic state, he stresses their submission to the commands of the authority. He gives a great deal of attention to the stress his subjects experience, and he notes how the strain of stress, rather than leading to disobedience, usually becomes translated into physical expressions, which reduce the experience of emotional stress:

> Conversion of psychological stress into physical symptoms is a commonly observed phenomenon in psychiatric practice. Ordinarily, there is improvement in the emotional state of the patient as the psychic stress comes to be absorbed by physical symptoms. Within this experiment, we can observe numerous signs of stress: sweating, trembling, and, in some instances, anxious laughter. Such physical expression not only indicate the presence of strain, but also reduce it. (161)

Milgram is a careful observer of his subjects, and his attention to the stress his subjects experience is something that I want to discuss at some length later. While Milgram gives rich attention to stress, he is not a careful observer of how his subjects respond to the problem of meaning. He shows some phenomenological interest in his subjects, but he does not carefully explore the meanings they form as they respond to the experimenter's demand.

Milgram argued that most of his subjects did not want to carry out the teacher's demand. When subjects in a similar experiment were simply asked to deliver shocks at levels they themselves found fit, the vast majority of people administered very low shocks. Milgram used this experiment to show that the high level of lethal shocks was not caused by any innate aggression on the part of the subjects. In this other, differently structured experiment, "There was an order of magnitude difference," Milgram explains (167).

Why is it that people who are free to do what they want, and know what they want, are somehow strangely compelled to do what someone else wants? In many subjects, the drama of the conflict between the students' desire and the teacher's desire was very intense. Students expressed feelings that they did not want to administer the shock, but even though they were, in theory, free to do as they wished, students could not act freely on their own desires.

The victim, about to be shocked, screams out in protest that he has heart trouble and may be killed. The student hears the actor's protest and hesitates. This hesitation was often very dramatic. For many experimental subjects, participation in the experiment caused considerable pain. One person, for example, complains loudly about what she is doing: "Must I go on? I'm worried about him. . . . Can't we stop? I'm shaking. I'm shaking. Do I have to go up there?" (80). Her shaking is fairly violent; she is suffering extreme agitation. When she describes her feelings later she says that she felt like she was "about to die." But when the authority tells her that she must continue with the experiment, she does so.

In one case, when the student points to the label on the shock generator that says "DANGER," the teacher reassures the student with his knowledge. The shocks are painful, he admits, but they cause no permanent tissue damage. The student accepts the teacher's knowledge and administers another shock when the meter on the generator reads 440 volts. Repeatedly, in the transcripts of these experiments, we find the student stopping and hesitating. This hesitation, however, is repeatedly overcome by the teacher's demand. All the teacher needs to say is, "The experiment must continue," and it does.

What goes on in students' minds when they listen to the teacher's explanation and then pull the lever to deliver the shock? Milgram says simply that the subjects are obedient.

Milgram describes the subject's obedience as a very passive capitulation to the demands of a leader:

> The most common adjustment of thought in the obedient subject is for
> him to see himself as not responsible for his own actions. He divests
> himself of responsibility by attributing all initiative to the experi-
> menter, a legitimate authority. He sees himself not as a person acting
> in a morally accountable way but as the agent of the external authority.
> (7–8)

In Milgram's judgment, the experiment triggers obedience as a kind of passive acceptance of demands that are not fully endorsed but are accepted as somehow necessary.

Lacanian theory offers a different account of what takes place in the experiment. Once we consider the experiment in relation to Lacanian theory, we place it within a framework of relationships between knowledge and desire. No longer a sociological and biological account of obedience, the experiment supports Lacan's account of the discourse of the master. In his theory of the four discourses, Lacan argues that knowledge always serves desire in some manner. Whenever the subject submits to the master's demand, knowledge is always a simple reflection of the master's desire. Subjects, under the pressure of demand, do not passively obey; they construct knowledge on the basis of the master's desire.

Milgram's own evidence suggests that obedient subjects are not passively submissive but active in the exercise of their orders. Obedience is, as Milgram points out, often initially charged with stress and ambivalence, but once there is submission, the subject's inner world of meaning converts an ugly job into an understanding of work that fulfills the subject's sense of purpose and personal dignity.

There is a great deal of evidence for this in the experiment, but Milgram's theoretical interests lie elsewhere. One subject Milgram describes shows an "appreciation for the help [he is given in learning how to work the machine] and a willingness to do what is required" (45). At the end of the experiment, the subject says "how honored he has been to help" (47). In a questionnaire returned by the subject several months later, he says that he was "not at all bothered" that the victim may have gotten painful shocks, and he says that "he believes more experiments of this sort should be carried out" (47). Milgram treats this subject as a kind of outrageous curiosity, quoting one observer who described this man as a "crude mesomorph of obviously limited intelligence" (45).

Milgram fails to take seriously the subject's observation before he learned the true nature of the experiment that he felt honored to have participated. This glimpse we have into a subject who obeys not passively but enthusiastically, who feels "not at all bothered" by hurting other people, and who appreciates what he is taught to do, should prompt us to think more carefully about how knowledge and meaning are generated by the pressure of demand.

Milgram wrestles constantly with the question of why people do what they do not want to do in the experiment. His answer to this question is simply that people are obedient, but there is clearly another very different possible answer. From a Lacanian perspective and from the evidence collected by Milgram himself, we might say that people confronted with emotional conflict do not slip easily into a grudging but passive obedience. Instead, subjects generate meanings, in effect, understandings or knowledge, that resolve their emotional conflict. Faced with different facts, the evidence of great pain felt by the student and great demand on the part of the experiment, subjects "understand" what they must do.

Catherine Belsey observes, "Ideology, masquerading as coherence and plenitude, is in reality inconsistent, limited, contradictory" (362). One problem in ideology is the need to explain how painfully lived contradictions become driven into the unconscious and made unavailable for thought. The Milgram experiment answers this question by showing how people, presented with contradictory demands for knowledge, solve the problem of knowledge by simply repressing contradiction.

In the experiment, the teacher says, "The experiment requires that you continue. . . . " (73). Students deliver the shock because they *understand* that the experiment must continue. Experimental subjects are clearly very much under stress when they respond to the conflicting cues of their situation. The student shows great pain; the teacher ignores this pain. The student is torn between two different identifications and can identify with the one who suffers and act on this knowledge, or the student can identify with, and submit to, the authority of the experimenter. This conflict in the students disappears, however, when they understand what must be done. For most people, unfortunately, understanding at this moment functions as massive repression. The pain of another person, the victim, becomes oddly absent to experience when students begin to understand their work in relation to the knowledge claims formulated by the teacher.[5]

Milgram never focuses carefully on meanings generated in these moments of capitulation. Most of his analysis of obedience is from the perspective of students who before obedience feel great stress, and afterward learn that their actions were morally compromised. Nonetheless, Milgram's narratives give insight into how different students respond to the teacher's demands.

Disobedient students do not massively repress the evidence of their senses. In one case, the teacher says, "It's absolutely essential to the experiment that we continue" (48). A disobedient student responds by saying, "I understand that statement, but I don't understand why the experiment is placed above this person's life" (45). The teacher answers this question about understanding with the reply, "There is no permanent tissue damage" (48). The disobedient student responds, "Well that's your opinion" (48). What we see in disobedience is subjects' rejection of an understanding for what they are asked to perform. Disobedient subjects instead are able to ask a series of questions that lead eventually to a clear understanding that the teacher's insistence is immoral. When there is a clear sense of contradiction between the demands of the authority and the evidence of the experiment, the student walks away from the experiment.

Obedient subjects, in contrast, are unable to pursue a line of thought that fully makes present, or makes sense, of the conflict they experience. In Milgram's data, for example, one female subject hesitates. The teacher remarks that "although the shocks are painful they cause no permanent tissue damage" (77). Milgram says, "She accepts the experimenter's comment" (77). We need to ask, "Why does she accept this?" What act of obedience is involved in this acceptance?

There clearly is a lot of information present in the field of this subject's experience. There is a machine with written categories of shock that begin with "SLIGHT SHOCK" and conclude with "DANGER—SEVERE SHOCK", there is a man screaming in a chair, and there is an experimenter's assurance of no permanent tissue damage. Why does the subject believe this assurance?

Clearly, this assurance can work only if she denies the evidence in front of her, only if she believes the teacher in an enormous leap of faith. She makes this leap, but she can do this only if there is a massive repression of the other information that troubles her. This is Lacan's argument about the belief generated by the discourse of the master. There is a belief, a real understanding that takes place, which is generated precisely by a massive repression of other conflicting information. The subject accepts the teacher's explanation only because she is able to repress that information that conflicts with what the teacher says. Her understanding frees her from conflict and hesitation. This understanding, this belief event, is so irrational that Milgram never considers it as a rational explanation for the obedience he finds. Nonetheless, the evidence suggests that this understanding is an important component of the response to demand.

In cult groups, we see how unconventional ideas can be subjects for firm and sacred belief. We quickly see these unconventional beliefs in others, but we seldom accept the possibility that these beliefs are the daily effects of masters who teach us to understand all manner of social, political, and psychological events in repressive ways. Most of us, as scholars, take part in academic conferences where understanding is, in theory, the most important goal of the social event. Yet, too often, many questions that would continue the complexity of an understanding are dismissed at conferences with simple demands such as those used by the teachers in Milgram's experiment. These demands, in response to crucial questions, do not answer the question, but they silence the person who asks the question. This Lacanian idea that understanding can be an effect of massive repression is similar to many ideas of poststructuralist theory and resembles Paul De-Man's argument in *Blindness and Insight* that every insight is an effect of structured blindness. Lacan's idea offers a more specific understanding, one that connects the repression first to the generation of understanding and second to a desire to please a master. Much of the argument of this book explores the implications of this kind of understanding and seeks ways to reveal and make public its insidious action.

In the Milgram experiment, understanding is a simple act of belief, a false representation generated in the student's mind by conflicted moral demands. Nonetheless, this understanding is a powerful force in the context of the experiment. It is that which is generated so that students need not respond to, make use of, or act on the freedom of thought they have. Through repressive understanding, the demanded action moves toward closure and becomes morally correct. This contrasts sharply with the actions of disobedient subjects who generate a dialectic through their persistent questions that lead to rebellion.

Understanding provides obedient students with an experience of doing the right thing, even though the action is morally reprehensible. Milgram observes that "administering shocks to the victim is incompatible with the self-image of many subjects. They do not readily view themselves as callous individuals capable of hurting another person" (156). As the experiment develops, this contrast between the idealized self and the actual self generates stress. In response to this stress, students make adjustments in the representations they have of themselves. They do not represent themselves as pawns of a sadistic experimenter. They are not the passive effects of someone's else will but the active heroes of their own will. They represent themselves as participating in a necessary experiment. They, in a very literal way, make sense within their bodies of what is happening. They come to develop a certain feeling about what they are doing, which precisely is an *understanding* that grounds their action in something they can avow to be true.

Under the pressure of demand, these people modify their understandings of who they are and what they must do. There are many and various formations that allow this. One man says, "I figured: Well this is an experiment, and Yale knows what's going on, and if they think it's all right, well, it's all right with me" (88). Some subjects come to believe that the pursuit of scientific knowledge requires sacrifices, while other subjects simply deny that the generator delivers dangerous shocks. What we see in all cases is that the representations generated by compliant students are modified by demand. In all cases, the net effect of demand, whatever effect its particular form of understanding takes, enforces the teacher's desire. The students are, in principle, free to act on their own different desire, but the effect of demand prompts students to feel that they, in fact, desire what the experimenter desires.

One-third of the experimental subjects became disobedient at some point in the experiment. These people simply refused to do what the experimenter asked. When they were asked to administer lethal shocks, they were able to say freely something like, "I do not have to do what you tell me to do," or, "I will not do so." These subjects were people who knew their own desire and were able to act on it. If I say, however, that these people were people who knew their own desire, I should emphasize that it is not simply that these subjects *have* their own desire. Their desire is a complex responsiveness to desire in the social field. What these subjects have as their own desire is a response to someone else's desire, and what is crucial is the ability of the experimental subject to respond freely to another. By respond freely, I mean a response that overcomes the constraints of an authority who seeks to suppress expressions of desire circulating in the social field. The people who refuse to deliver the lethal shock are people who respond to the desire of a person who has been excluded and oppressed by the authority figure. Only a small group of subjects, however, was able to do this. The majority of the subjects, lacking a democratic flexibility in desire, obeyed the authority.

In contrast to the humanist claim that each individual has an autonomous desire that responds freely to social truth claims, the Milgram experiment suggests that most people operate not on their own desires but on the desires of particular others in authority. The use of demand in teaching, then, is not something always doomed to failure. Typically, I think, it will encounter tenacious resistance in students with attachments to conflicting demand beliefs, but it may also introduce material that is, for the moment anyway, readily adopted by some students. Indeed, the Milgram experiment suggests that demand, in optimum contexts, is frequently successful. As I argue in the next chapter, however, demand is not a solution to social problems; it is a problem that requires a solution.

Teresa Ebert argued that subjects who learn to express their desires freely generate social oppression. In order to remedy social problems, she suggested that limitations on free expression could be good practice. This limitation should be an effect of responsible knowledge practices that alter the representations students have of their lives. Through such altered representations, Ebert sought to recover real, more honest social relations. The Milgram experiment would seem to turn Ebert's argument on its head. Real social relations may not be improved by authoritative knowledge practices that represent other people by suppressing the free expression of human desire. Indeed, knowledge practices may convert honest direct relations with real people into manipulative relations with abstractions.

Demand and Cultural Formation

An understanding of demand allows us to consider the issue of free speech from a more comprehensive perspective than its immediate effects. Demand, considered from this broader perspective, does not simply facilitate particular truth effects; it also structures a specific set of libidinal relations between subjects. These libidinal relations, and not the meaning of the signifiers that circulate in the relations, determine the role discourse plays in society. The acceptance of a truth that circulates by the force of demand circulates at the costly price of the suppression of spontaneous flows of desire and anxiety generated by real people in real-world conditions.

People will be responsible for the needs of others only when they are responsive to the feelings of need, anxiety, and desire in real other people who work in real material conditions. This direct response will take place only when people are fully responsive to, and fully responsible for, their own feelings. This responsibility for individual feeling, for full complexity and depth of individual feeling, is thus of political not simply personal importance.

Consider Ebert's emphasis on the distinction between need and demand. Evidence indicates that democratic societies on the whole most effectively satisfy need. The Nobel Prize–winning Indian economist Amartya Sen has recently argued that no famine has ever occurred in a democratic society. As a former Peace Corps volunteer to India during a time of famine, I feel considerable hesitation in fully accepting Sen's claim. Nonetheless, Sen's book, *Development as Freedom,* makes a strong case for freedom of speech as an important facilitator for the distribution of objects of need. Totalitarian governments of all types are typically insensitive to both human need and human desire. Human actions that are needed to alleviate famine are rendered ineffective by totalitarian governments. It is as if all the small relations (small expressions of desire) existing between people that need to be organized to plant crops and distribute relief were disrupted. The totalitarian government imposes its own order as a reflection of its own representations of the truth of the world condition. Democratic societies, in contrast, seek to find some fair stance in relation to the different claims of need and desire generated by their citizens.[6]

Ebert's pedagogy implies that a received truth about others will establish real relations between people. It should be clear, however, that direct relations between people will not be supported by authorities who, for whatever conscious reason, act to represent other people for their followers according to some frozen formula of representation termed *knowledge.* Once relations between people are established by established truths that circulate by demand, real relations between people disappear. Real relations vanish because real expressions of desire vanish. Oppression will be countered when people's feelings of repression find responsible recognition, which does not take place from top-down transmissions of truth. This takes place from bottom-up responsiveness to real people speaking in social contexts in which their speech is not easily silenced by political authorities. Responsiveness to others, however, is a complex task.

The Milgram experiment suggests that sensitivity, or empathy, is not a solution to the problem of suffering. Milgram describes "a woman of hysterical tendencies," who very much feels the pain the victim experiences (84). She wants to terminate the experiment, but her need to please and be loved by an authority is greater than her desire to avoid harming another person. Thus she obeys orders, though painfully. Milgram's description of hysterical women is sexist; however, most subjects, men and women, either hysterically or obsessively chose a special (obedient) relation to an authority figure, even when they felt for the victim. What was crucial for justice was not simply a recognition that the victim suffered but a recognition that the rights of the victim were equal to the rights of the teacher.

Let me now advance an argument to support a posthumanist ideal of free speech.[7] I defend free speech in terms of a larger cultural perspective on the various mechanisms that generate and regulate subjectivity. What is important in teaching is not simply the truths advocated but the structures of discourse and subjectivity set into motion. Any society that relies purely on something termed *knowledge* will be oppressive. What is wrong, then, about a pedagogy of demand is not the immediate effect of a demand but the larger network of social relations structured by demand.

Demand creates a subject fully submissive to the meanings of the master. Gilbert Chaitin points out that demand replays the subject's most primitive relations between meaning and pleasure, relations in which the child's need to symbolize is supported (or not) by the mother's smile (169). The mother's smile, in itself, confers meaning on symbolization; it marks the meanings that really matter.[8] The Lacanian theorist Robert Samuels argues that the average social subject submits to demand, but this submission is costly. "In both hypnosis and love" (overly idealized love), he observes, "there is an idealization of the Other that serves to deplete the ego of its power and energy." (122–23). Society, in general, operates largely by means of the force of the demand. This is a demand made by culture as a whole, what Lacan terms the *Other,* the general expectations of society as they are present in a set of symbols and understandings. Samuels points out that subjectivity is to a large extent generated as the subject submits to the demand of the Other (90). The teacher who facilitates the circulation of truth by means of demand is thus a simple extension of normal social practice.[9]

The problem is that the "normal" creation of human subjects causes social problems. Because the normal subject of society is produced by a submission to the demand of the Other, the normal subject is robbed of a flexible response to feeling states both within the self and within others. Desires that arise from within particular selves are not mobilized for social interactions; desires that arise in others are not recognized. Individuals most determinedly constituted by demand are individuals whose desires are fixated by the practices of strong authorities. In this way, the social field suffers from an inability to transmit freely among different subject messages inflected with spontaneous expressions of desire.

The consequence of this state of affairs is both an impoverishment of the self (an inability to feel responsive to desire) and a symbolic rigidity in the social field. Individuals not nourished by free movements of desire become members of social groups quick to scapegoat others. They are anxious about the expression of desire and quick to vilify its unapproved forms. Characteristically, they see outside-group individuals with different desires than their own as threats to their own fixated desire.

Slavoj Žižek suggests that people who are robbed of their own relation to desire find the robbers of this desire elsewhere. Other people will be seen not simply as different but as enemies who threaten their well-being. In order to maintain their love for the Other who has stolen their desire, they will find external others to blame for the loss caused by their submission to the Other. In *Looking Awry*, Žižek argues that more so than democracies, it is the "fate" of "totalitarianism" to be "condemned ceaselessly to invent external 'enemies' to account for its failures" (168). Speech determined by demand may be more disposed to violence and exploitation than speech determined by unrestricted movements of desire. Speech determined by demand more violently misrepresents others because it is a form of speech generated by a subject threatened by the desires of others. It thus more anxiously seeks to displace the various threats to its master's truth. Real other people, people such as the victims in Milgram's experiment, serve as simple and empty representations for their fear or ambition.

I should make it clear that I am not developing an argument in support of an autonomous subject. The point that I want to make is precisely that speech and desire are socially determined by mechanisms in the social field, but such a generalization does not go far enough.

In the Milgram experiment, if we ask what goes wrong in the flow of a message from one who suffers to those able to help, the answer would seem to be that what goes wrong is an understanding. The victim's plea for help is ignored because someone understands that it is not relevant to his purpose. Let me extrapolate from this to suggest a larger generalization: People suffer because various kinds of understandings make this suffering seem necessary or inevitable, or even desirable. These understandings, moreover, are held in place by authorities who demand belief from their followers. In this manner, abstract political claims made about others become more important than the information generated by direct expressions of desire or need generated by real people in real, material conditions.

To say that desire is socially constructed does not mean that desire should be socially constructed on the basis of some enlightened social plan. The general social field is constantly responding to changes in cultural conditions, material conditions, and technological innovation. Human desire must be able respond to these changes in its diversity without censorship or misrepresentation. Human desire must be able to flow freely across a symbolic field.

This analysis suggests, then, that demand is not the solution to political problems. Demand, rather than the solution to a problem, is itself the problem. Alternative pedagogies would seek to create societies in which the free transmission of expressed desire is not only possible but privileged.

4 Desire as Agency
The Ethics and Politics of Composition

In my previous two chapters, I explored two different postmodernist strategies for teaching. One strategy, developed by Berlin, seeks to use debate to explore and overcome ideological positions. Another strategy, formulated by Ebert, uses the teacher's authority to promote a truth. Both of these formulas have serious limitations. Berlin's strategy fails to recognize that human subjects have fixated beliefs that are not responsive to rational debate. Ebert's strategy, whatever the value of its ideology, fails to produce a subject who is responsive to bottom-up perceptions of human suffering. It risks producing a Stalinist society in which the truth of social experience is whatever any master wants to say it is. If millions of farmers starve from poor potato harvests, this reality can be annulled by an official discourse that teaches an idealized truth. I use Stalin as an example, but any ideology quickly becomes a belief structure that preserves the status quo and the power of those who teach the beliefs. Organized political groups are necessary for social action, but fixated ideologies are inimical to social justice.

Both debate and authoritative declarations are modes of discourse that impede the circulation and understanding of human desire. These forms of discourse may be expressions of particular desires or defenses of particular desires, but they do not participate in the necessary circulation of desire within a human community. An ideal community would respond to expressions of suffering from different individuals at the peripheries of the center of power. This ideal response requires the movement of this expression of suffering along a chain of signification from the person involved to a reporter, to a medium such as television, to an audience comprising many members of that society. In this way, crucial information about who suffers becomes public knowledge.

This ideal society that offers immediate and equal opportunities for the expression of need requires development in two ways. First, there must be a genuine free circulation of desire in a community. This involves a commitment to equal opportunities for the expression and communication of emotion for all people. Most important, we must find ways to experience and respond in an ethically responsible manner to the emotions of those who, as an effect of ideological practice, have been excluded from this dialogue. If, as Butler, Laclau, and Žhižek agree in *Contingency, Hegemony, Universality,* the normal discursive practice of any culture characteristically requires the "exclusion of certain contents from any given version of universality" (137), then efforts must be made to recover for signification what has been excluded, repressed, and foreclosed.

This circulation of excluded information becomes even more complex when many different people or groups of people with different degrees of suffering and different discourses compete within a social body for attention and support. Adequate response to these multiple requests requires sorting the information received, making decisions about who is most needy, and formulating effective responsive strategies. Just as there must develop more opportunities for marginalized people to speak for themselves, there must develop an increased elasticity in acts of identification that respond to the appeals of others. This elasticity involves the development, as I suggested earlier, of an anti-ideological identity. What we see in the Milgram experiment is the effectiveness by which masters are able to explain the suffering of others as necessary or unimportant. As long as normal patterns of identification and normal conditions of hegemony require massive submissions to a master, political understandings will entail oppression.[1]

Within a particular social group, individuals are able to make dramatic sacrifices for the benefit of group members. We need only think of the enormous outpouring of sympathy for the survivors of the Oklahoma City bombing and survivors of natural disasters that are aided by media appeals for help and government programs. Sacrifices, however, are very difficult to generate for those in outside-group status. Categories of *outside-group* and *inside-group,* however, are defined by masters, and if we can be less submissive in our use of master discourses, we can be more inclusive of the voices of others.

In this chapter, I explore how different attitudes toward writing set in motion different responses to the forces of desire in discourse. Writing always responds to multiple masters and thus always contains possibilities for undoing the force of a particular master (and that ideology) by bringing into consciousness repressed and ambivalent modes of thinking and feeling denied by the master. Children ideally learn to respond to the differing desires of both parents, to find their own complicated feelings as something other than a simple assumption of what someone else wants for them.[2] Students in writing ideally learn to respond to the complex diversity of social space, making sense of their own place in relation to it. In this discussion, I take a very broad view of the history and theory of rhetoric. I begin with Plato, survey traditional ideas about composition, and conclude with a complicated theory of the function of desire in discourse as found in the work of Lacan.

On the Knowledge of Writing

The discipline of composition has always held a problematic status in academia. In "Gorgias," Plato criticized the early composition practitioners, the Greek rhetoricians, for lacking any kind of knowledge that could be taught, and he compared the art of rhetoric to the art of flattery. Flattery can take many forms, but it always involves some relation to desire, and it usually implies a submissive relation to the desire of another. Aristotle was somewhat more optimistic, suggesting that rhetoric involved not only pathos, or playing on the emotions of the audience, but also ethos, or fostering an identification of the audience with the speaker. It seems to me that Aristotle, with his more complicated view of a desire set in circulation by rhetoric, got it right, but the field of rhetoric and composition has never been clear regarding how it works to mobilize and circulate desire.

Since Plato, there have been many attempts to define the knowledge that composition confers, but even a cursory perusal of contemporary work in composition theory indicates that we are still very much unsure about exactly what we do. I suggest that Plato's assertion that rhetoric is the art of flattery is a better description of what actually goes on in teaching than most of us would like to admit. I also think that now, more than ever, it is important to understand how desire is set in motion by classroom practices. Now that composition studies has become a program in multicultural awareness and dialogue, it is important to understand in a careful and systematic way how writing can generate and fashion desire as it responds to multiple centers of authority and attention.

Composition, more so than any other discipline, requires a "proper" response to the desires of others. It requires students to produce new textual representations of themselves that satisfy the desires of their teachers, textbooks, and peer readers. Erika Lindemann observes that "unless students can anticipate what constitutes a successful response to an assignment, they will continue to write poorly" (202). As teachers, we have a responsibility to understand what we mean when we ask a student to take responsibility for a "successful response." We need to consider, in a careful and systematic manner, what it means for students, as writers, to develop a kind of double consciousness, to think not only of what they think but also of what others will think. What position do we put our students in when we ask them, in Lindemann's description, to anticipate the response of an audience persistently, seeking always to give it something that will satisfy.

James Moffett has argued that teaching composition, unlike the teaching of any other subject in the university, involves a reversal of most of our assumptions about teaching. In other disciplines, we use language to teach a subject. In composition, we teach the use of the language itself. "English, mathematics, and foreign languages are not about anything in the same sense that history, biology, physics and other primarily empirical subjects are about something," Moffett argues. "English, French, and mathematics are symbol systems. . . . When a student learns one of these systems, he *learns how* to operate it" (6).

Instruction in the *proper use* of a language, which one already *uses* as a native speaker, unlike other university subjects, is a training of desire. As I demonstrate at some length, composition is an operation in the production, prohibition, negotiation, and reformulation of desire. Most teachers would claim that they judge products, processes, or skills—anything but desire. But the better we understand how these things manipulate desire, the better we will be able to formulate a theory and an ethics of teaching composition.

Work in Composition as the Production of Desire

Writing instruction from the Renaissance onward has linked writing to a practice of imitation whereby certain admired texts or admired styles of subjectivity become models for the kind of "work" that must be produced. Through proper "work" a student shows a certain "skill" or "intelligence." Jim Kinneavy points out that in the Middle Ages, the study of grammar included as its "main concern" the reading and study of "literary texts" (8). The assumption operating here is that the study of great texts leads to the production of good writing. The word *study* is used here in a somewhat disingenuous way, because when students are asked to study a text, they are really asked to admire it. The assumption seems to be that as the work of study leads to the experience of admiration, the experience of admiration leads to forms of expression that successfully imitate or recover some ideal pattern found in the original. In this manner, something experienced as value in the model text is taken in by the writer, carried into the composition process, and redelivered in some new but recognizable form in the final written product.

The study of great literature as a contribution to the development of good writing is not an antiquated model for teaching writing; this model continues to operate. Such models of writing instruction are no longer as popular as they once were, but the use of admired texts as a basis or rationale for writing instruction continues. Most teachers no longer honor a single culturally enshrined tradition that embodies all that is best in human experience. Instead, teachers promote something only slightly different: having their own valued texts that serve to initiate and define a proper use of language. Joseph Harris observes that most of us do not know much about what goes on when people teach writing. When we look at published accounts of teaching, Harris points out, scholars commonly "present [their] own reading of a text as a classroom 'discussion'" (788). Typically, Harris claims, "while many students in the class do seem to be working hard, what they mostly seem to be working *at* is trying to figure out what their teacher wants them to say" (789). In writing classes, now as before, a text serves as a motive for a series of responses that get at what a teacher *wants*. This want is generated by study and leads to a discipline of work that results in a written product.

David Bartholomae, in "What is Composition and (if you know what that is) Why Do We Teach It?," observes that there is an "array of often competing desires for order and control" in writing instruction (11). In an essay that explores what it might mean to practice composition in the context of contemporary postmodernist culture, Bartholomae describes and examines various goals of composition. After characterizing composition as a "diffuse set of practices and desires," (11) Bartholomae concludes his essay by speaking his own desire, "We can imagine that the goal of writing instruction might be to teach an act of criticism that would enable a writer to interrogate his or her own text in relationship to the problems of writing and the problems of disciplinary knowledge" (17). Bartholomae boldly dismisses a previously accepted composition goal (an orderly and masterful text) and puts forward a different goal: the production of a less orderly text working against its own desire for mastery, power, and knowledge. Later in this essay I want to talk in more detail about what it might mean to develop a desire that would counter the more common desire for mastery, power, and knowledge. For now, however, let me emphasize, once again, how composition practices become exercises in generating and fashioning desire.

Bartholomae's goal for composition clearly reveals an attempt to direct the movement of desire. He also wants his students to want to perform what he describes as a rejection of desire for mastery. He wants students to exhibit "an interrogation" of their own text. Students will be evaluated on the basis of how well they can show that they want what Bartholomae wants. Yet even though this complex circulation of desire is obvious in Bartholomae's essay, present in the language of his analysis of composition, nowhere is it given systematic attention. The manipulation of desire is instead represented in terms of a simple skill that must be taught, an "act of criticism." Here, as elsewhere in composition theory, desire is vigorously appealed to while it remains strangely invisible. Desire is named, but it is not recognized. It is the unconscious of composition theory; it operates everywhere; it is constantly spoken; but it is effectively ignored through multiple means of defense.

Bartholomae wants his students to practice composition as an exercise in proper desire. His desire to rebel against the desire for mastery is presented as an objective principle of measurement in composition. It helps to define the work writers must demonstrate. Bartholomae's own desire is disguised as an apparently rational principle that would shape communal goals for composition. For the last fifty years, this kind of representation of the writer's task has been largely accepted. As writing courses become increasingly linked to cultural studies, however, we can no longer ignore the role desire plays in writing. We must understand how an act of criticism functions to generate and complicate desire. As I discuss later, cultural studies, more so than traditional approaches to writing, confronts and evaluates desire. Because this confrontation now takes place more directly than ever before, we need to understand what we are doing. We need to understand desire as a distinctive element that performs an essential role in writing and in the larger contexts of culture and subjectivity.

Flattery is not always an obvious factor in writing, but it is always present. It is part of a complex circuit of desire whereby student work is judged in relation to the verbal objects admired or desired by their teachers. In teaching composition, we inevitably seem to advocate certain styles of subjectivity. Skill in writing is not a matter of rote memorization; it does not require an assimilation of important facts; and it is not, Linda Flower's important work notwithstanding, a matter primarily of solving problems in an objective manner.

While everyone is, in theory, free to compose as they wish, evaluation in composition appeals to familiar principles that measure a work's success. Skill in writing seems to involve the development of an elusive skill in assimilating, embedding, and relating bits of language. But how is this development evaluated? Good writing has form, style, coherence, and an awareness of its audience. What are these things, and how do they operate in the act of composition? Form, style, coherence, and audience are not objective qualities; they are themselves covert modes for the training of desire. Perhaps more important, this training that is most central to the real *work* of composition is also most unconscious.

In contrast to learning some privileged factual content, writing requires an act of composition. What makes this aspect of composition particularly difficult to understand and evaluate is that it draws on, and responds to, complex and dynamic nodes of desire that select, order, and give value to the material of language. What we call *writing style*—word choice, tone, and structural relationships between words—may seem objective elements of writing. But style is never a simple conformity to correct rules for writing. It develops from imitation, but it usually develops unconsciously. It is expressed at some elusive level of self-awareness, where the desire of a writer finds its own form in language.

Form, like style, involves choice, and wherever there is choice that is evaluated, there is an exercise in the training of desire. Form in writing can be present in many ways. It may be central to an assignment, such as when students are assigned argumentative papers. In this case, students, whatever they may want to do as writers, must discipline their behavior so that they give the teacher the correct "form"—what the teacher wants. Consider for a moment how this kind of exercise disciplines desire.

Back in the mid-1970s, when I taught a version of James Kinneavy's aims-and-modes approach to composition at the University of Texas, many of my students would receives C's on papers because, although they set out with the intention of writing the informative papers I assigned, they ended up writing arguments or narrative essays. Once students got their papers back with my responses, they could quickly and easily see that, in fact, they did not write informative papers, and this was interesting. Even though they clearly knew what an informative paper was supposed to be (in some dimension of knowing that does not seem to connect fluidly to writing), they could not remember their need to perform my desire for a informative paper as their own papers began, sentence by sentence, to develop, speak, and respond to their own desires. Over time, their representation of my desire, held in memory, lost its relation to their acting selves. In this manner, they wrote what they did not want to write because they could not remember that their task was to give me what I wanted. Good students consistently remembered what they were supposed to want to do as writers, which means that they constantly policed their own desires (or found themselves in relation to their teacher's desires) as they produced the kind of document demanded.

In addition to form operating as genre, form operates as a principle of coherence. Form is the experience the reader has when it makes sense to connect one fragment of discourse to another. But how does this experience of sense come about? All we can say is that the connection gives satisfaction. Kenneth Burke argues "Form . . . is an arousing and fulfilling of desire. A work has form in so far as one part of it leads a reader to anticipate another part, to be gratified by the sequence" (124). Form thus is not in signification but in desire. In form, it is desire itself that is manipulated and shaped *in relation to* signification. To create an anticipation is to create a desire to know. Satisfaction is similarly responsive to desire: facts will not satisfy us unless we have been led to want them. Good writers can do this only if they know their audience; however, this shorthand term, *knowing*, obscures the acute conscious and unconscious responsiveness that alert writers develop in dialectical response to what other people want to know, hear, or feel.

When we link good writing to proper desire, we should consider the dialectical relations between desire and subjectivity put into motion. Subjectivity shapes desire as it sets it in motion, but desire also shapes subjectivity as it discovers itself in desire. Good writing, however, always reflects some particular model of desirable subjectivity. It is honest, insightful, or reasonable. What counts as a desirable subjectivity, however, has undergone historical revision as the experts who define good writing change their minds about how they want subjects to act. The writing assignments we require and the evaluations we give thus reflect changing historical assumptions we have about how good subjects should desire.

Lester Faigley argues that composition typically functions as a "disciplinary mode of control" for subjects and that "many of the conflicts within composition studies" reflect "larger cultural conflicts over the question of the subject" (225). For many years, we wanted authors to act like rational subjects and autonomous individuals. This Enlightenment idealization of the rational autonomous subject, however, later gave way to a view of subjectivity that was more embedded in social processes. In 1971, Kenneth Bruffee advocated what Faigley terms a *social subject* that works in a community and understands the socially constructed nature of knowledge (226). As writing teachers responded to this model of subjectivity, students were told to work in groups and to respond actively to each other as they constructed written texts. More recently, the emphasis on community and consensus has given rise to an appreciation of the heterogeneous and unstable nature of subjectivity. Much current postmodernist theory, seeking a political responsiveness to marginalized people, describes the subject, as Faigley observes, situated "among many competing discourses that precede the subject" (227) and advocates "openness to heterogeneity" (233) as a particularly desirable trait.

A curious feature of composition is that all the different models of privileged subjectivity require that students produce this particular model as the result of some kind of control over an almost infinite number of subtle selections of discourse choice and arrangement. This work of relating and embedding the discourse of others inevitably expresses a linguistic agency working in a sometimes reflective but more often spontaneous act of thinking and relating. Writing requires of the student an operation of linguistic agency and demands that the student control this agency. It sets up this task so that control most often eludes the management of the conscious mind, yet it demands that this control operate effectively.

Controlling the Desire of the Unconscious

We must examine more fully how instruction in composition trains and disciplines unconscious desire. Erika Lindemann observes, "prewriting, writing, and rewriting are concurrent activities, repeated over and over again as writers come progressively closer to resolving incongruities between what they intend to say and what the discourse actually says" (187). It is as if writers persisted in seeking to control what they intend in writing, but the act of intended control were constantly deflected by the materialization of words. Most frequently, writers rewrite an important essay very slowly, moving tangentially toward some degree of control over intentions that constantly go astray.

There is a measure of conscious choice and control in writing, but when we talk to students about their papers, we often find that many sentences, words, and even paragraphs are simply there, a product of the writing experience, but are not self-consciously chosen as part of some carefully crafted and fully intended construction. Much of writing, even much of good, carefully edited writing, is simply an accumulation of spontaneous expression. Students speak a language that simply comes to them from a realm beyond thought or planned intention. Perhaps more often, writing is intended in a careful and exact way, but the sequence of words that appears on paper are curiously and dependably pulled into directions that writers do not recognize until they become detached readers of their own written product.

Writing involves an almost impossible attempt to control an infinite number of largely spontaneous processes that are most often elusive and resistant to control. If we were to inquire about the kind of agency acting in this linkage of discourse fragments, it could be described only as some seemingly random expression of desire. It comes to us as if it were from a dream; it is where we find ourselves in language before we make any choice about language. Philosophers would say there is an 'intentionality' behind these acts, but this intentionality is enormously unconscious and difficult to control by means of conscious rational thought. Yet this enigmatic intentionality behind all our acts of composition is precisely what must be trained and disciplined by composition instruction. If students are anxious to know what the teacher wants, it may be in part because they, at some level, unconsciously intuit that tacitly and unconsciously imitating a teacher's desire is more important to successful writing than following the explicit directions given by teachers.

The problem of agency—the problem of disciplining the agency that produces successful academic work—is more central to the practice of composition than to any other academic discipline. Agency is more central to composition because composition makes the most irrational demands on agency. Composition, more so than other disciplines, demands control over acts that are normally beyond conscious control. Various arts, of course, use the unconscious and explore its depth for expression. Composition does this is as well, but it is often taught as a simple exercise in rational thought.

Composition characteristically requires not a rational act but a subtle, unconscious response to competing and inchoate intuitions and desires. When writers remember at a certain point in the development of an essay that they *need* more facts because their teachers have explicitly said so, they rely on unconscious processes to interrupt their more overt acts of consciousness. This, in fact, describes how good writing succeeds. As we seek to anticipate the responses of others, we interrupt and complicate what we ourselves want to do. Clearly, it is the desire of the other that must interrupt our relation to our own desire. This other desire must speak in us at a moment when we are most out of touch with it. It is in our unconscious acts more than in our following of any conscious rules that we sharpen what Flower calls "reader-based prose" (237).

The Agency of Writing and the Agency of Politics

Concerns for the politics of composition make the theme of desire more important than ever before. I have tried to suggest that the root of agency in composition is desire. Writing begins with desire that is mobilized at the level of an individualized memory, but this desire quickly becomes embedded in a social network of libidinized discourse. In response to this libidinized network, desire becomes part of a rhizomic set of social relations that respond to, and operate on, desire. Desire becomes something anticipated, negotiated, reformulated, and displaced. Composition practice thus works on desire, and this is part of the necessary work of composition. We might consider, however, that the work of politics is a similar process of recognizing, negotiating, reformulating, and displacing desire.

I want to describe how different theories of composition work on desire and further suggest how this work responds to different political goals.

Many scholars, following the lead of liberal theory, see desire as that which is, and should be, set in motion by discourse practice. Donald Murray, for example, asks students, much like an analyst, to free-associate as preparation for writing. He similarly suggests that students look at what they have done and find their own centers of "interest." There is much more of this material that I could cite from Murray, but the point is that Murray promotes intentional acts that set desire in motion. More important, Murray implicitly values the free expression of desire. Free association and student-centered responses guarantee that the act of writing is centered on students' personal relations to desire.[3]

Many practitioners of cultural studies, in contrast, are suspicious of a pedagogy privileging the free expression of desire. Teresa Ebert argues that pedagogies that emphasize desire involve an "erasure of the class struggle through post-alizing desire [i.e., desire defined by various new theories, such as poststructuralism, postmodernism, post-Lacanian psychoanalysis, and postgay queer theory]. The post-al theory of desire is, in effect, a new justification for the desires of those who have and an erasure of the needs of others as basically unreal" (811). Lynn Worsham usefully points out that Ebert's sharp distinction between Marxist truth and post-al desire "suggests a rather undialectical relation to so called post-al theories that refuses to recognize that history also happens in these theories, that they too may have their moment of 'truth'" (218). The attention Ebert gives to the reality of real human need is important; her dismissal of desire, however, is shortsighted.

It is not fully clear to me how Ebert's pedagogy would work. She argues that "critique is not judgment, but explanation" (812). She insists in "For a Red Pedagogy" that her project is simply a mode of knowing. Yet her knowing and her explanations of desire emphatically seek to change desire, to insist that it take only fully sanctioned forms.

If the liberal dialogical attitude toward the desiring subject can reproduce a capitalist ideology, the cultural-studies attitude toward the desiring subject can reproduce a Stalinist ideology. If political action does not recognize the desiring subject as the essential factor of political life, then political action will express nothing more than the sheer brutal force of political will.

Ebert argues that desire should not be freely expressed because power controls desire, and the dominant desires are the effect of a dominant power. The work of Judith Butler, in *The Psychic Life of Power,* and of Slavoj Žižek, in *The Sublime Object of Ideology,* encourages us to turn this argument on its head to consider an opposite idea. It is not power that determines desire but desire that determines power.

Lacan's theory of the four discourses suggests more complex generalizations. As I will discuss more fully in the next chapter, power can determine desire, as when the discourse of the master controls desire in the follower, but this determination of desire is curiously secondary. It is the derivative of a more primary desire to relate, to love, and to be loved. The

desires for love and recognition have the potential to create just and equitable communities. The desires generated by masters, in contrast, require
repression. Blind attachment to forms of repression blindly generates imaginary enemies. Masters, their discourses and their desires, are thus generally counterproductive to the formation of equitable communities.[4]

Pedagogies for the Circulation of Desire

If desire is the key motive behind human action, in both writing and politics, we must understand how composition, as it works on desire, can contribute to the work of democratic politics. An important first step in this
understanding is to recognize that desire, more so than need, is the central
fabric of politics. That is, humans characteristically follow desire and not
need in their expression of, and response to, politics. For example, people
often suffer hunger (denial of biological need) to have a socially acceptable
body; they suffer death to preserve a state that represents their desired
identity; and they deny sexuality to serve a church. All this behavior and
countless other examples show that need keeps the biological body alive,
but desire keeps the body of identity alive. For most people, the body of
identity is more important than the body of biology. As politicians have
long known, people will gladly suffer physical deprivation and kill their
neighbors for little more than a need for a symbolic identity.

Deleuze and Guattari suggest that problems in ideology can be understood as problems in desire (104). They envision desire operating in terms
of a circuit between subjects and a variety of objects: other subjects, technological objects, even animals. This theoretical perspective gives useful
emphasis to the generation and circulation of desire within a social body.
Lacanian theory, in contrast, more effectively describes blockages and im-
prisonments of desire. In *Looking Awry*, Slavoj Žižek points out that desire
can operate in terms of pathological attachments that restrict the free flow
of desire and thus constrain both discourse and the recognition of desires
in others and in oneself.

Culture and human subjectivity constitute a complex mechanism in-
volving circuits and processes for the production, transmission, reduction,
and amplification of desire. Cultural activities employ various devices that
manage desire through the use of generating agents, blocking agents, and
intersubjective and technological relations. In a democratic society, people
make choices as they consciously or unconsciously express their desires. In
an ideal democracy, people express their own desires in some ethical relation to the desires of others. An ideal democracy requires that people be
able to recognize their own desires and those of others. In both cases, desire must circulate freely within and among people. Oppression results

whenever desires are cut off from expression and circulation. Victor Vitanza, in "Concerning a Postclassical Ethos as Para/Rhetorical Ethics, the 'Selphs' and The Excluded Third," argues that "a non-oppressive politics is impossible unless and until there is a 'paraethical politics'—by which [he means] a condition for a politics informed by (free-flowing) desires" (395).

In order to envision a society in which justice is desired rather than imposed, we must understand how desire flows and circulates in a culture. How does culture generate desire? How is it passed from one individual to another? How does it develop mobility and individualized permutations? Conversely, what factors prevent the circulation of desire? How is it that some desires generated by some desiring individuals can be defined by culture as undesirable?

Lacan's four discourses offer an informative representation of relationships among desire, the unconscious, value, and knowledge.[5] Lacan claims that desire, as agency, produces four distinctly different discourses. This four-discourse theory, similar in some ways to the theory put forward by James Kinneavy twenty years ago, can help composition theory better understand how the circulation of desire, put into motion by discourse use, can contribute to democratic cultural practices. The four discourses— master, university, hysteric, and analyst—help explain three important factors. First, they describe how desire is generated and circulated by cultural authority. Second, they describe how desire becomes fixated and resistant to dialogic mediation. Third, they suggest that discourse cannot operate as agency except in and through desire.

Lacan defines each discourse in terms of a mathematical-like formula he terms a *matheme*. These mathemes can be frustrating to read; nonetheless, they are helpful metaphors that show condensed relationships quickly. I provide these mathemes and offer some instruction in reading them.

The four discourses are:

$$\frac{S_1}{\$} \rightarrow \frac{S_2}{a} \quad \text{master discourse}$$

$$\frac{\$}{a} \rightarrow \frac{S_1}{S_2} \quad \text{hysteric discourse}$$

$$\frac{S_2}{S_1} \rightarrow \frac{a}{\$} \quad \text{university discourse}$$

$$\frac{a}{S_2} \rightarrow \frac{\$}{S_1} \quad \text{analyst discourse}$$

I want to emphasize one important aspect of this representation. Discourse can effect different relations among knowledge, desire, and value, but the agency of this effect is not a pure expression of signification. It is an effect of repression and desire as these elements take particular places in discourse. A quick look at the mathemes shows that the *objet a,* loosely defined as surplus desire, can take four positions in four different modes of discourse.[6] The figure $ signifies a divided subject who has spoken desires that are both conscious and unconscious. The line that separates the top element from the bottom element is the bar of repression. The arrow that connects the two sets of elements suggests that the elements on the left function as structures for the production of a discourse effect when the receiving elements on the right take the positions shown.

Lacan's theory of four discourses resembles Jim Kinneavy's theory of the four discourses. I can refer to two of these discourses, that of the master and that of the university, to explain how the *objet a,* or the place of desire in discourse, serves to determine the effect of a discourse. Jim Kinneavy argued that two important discourses were informative discourse and persuasive discourse. In Lacan's theory, the master discourse corresponds closely to persuasive discourse as it fixes desire in relation to knowledge, and university discourse corresponds to informative discourse as it is concerned purely with the transmission of knowledge. I want to emphasize how discourse functions depend on how desire functions in a divided subject. University discourse works only when subjects desire to put aside their real desires, to serve as keepers or transmitters for signification. Persuasion, on the other hand, works when subjects desire to put aside their divided nature to promote a potentially disputable truth.

Both Butler and Žižek have argued that power is supported by enjoyment. Lacan's theory of the four discourses indicates that power and enjoyment are linked not simply to each other but also to knowledge and defensive symptoms in terms of which individuals irrationally maintain their attachments to an oppressive ideology. This oppression, then, is supported by the pleasures of identification they cannot (literally) suffer to give up.

The discourse of the master is:

$$\frac{S_1}{\$} \longrightarrow \frac{S_2}{a}$$

The left-hand set of terms designates factors active in the subject who produces a discourse, and the right-hand set of terms designates factors active in the subject who listens. The arrow that connects the two terms, one on the left and one on the right, can be read as a representation of a message sent by a speaker to a receiver:

Speaker ➤ Receiver

There are not only two sides but there are also two signifiers given on each side. Each signifier, wherever it may be, is in one of four positions (top-left, bottom-left, top-right, bottom-right). The signifiers are meaning-ful but so are their positions. The meaning of the positions is read as follows:

$$\frac{\text{agent}}{\text{truth}} \rightarrow \frac{\text{Other}}{\text{production}}$$

Thus, on the top level, we find an *agent* for discourse sending a message to an other on the right. This designation is important because the agency is not the person but the element (a signifier or a structure of desire) functioning in discourse.

Each of four signifiers (S1, S2, a, $) can be in each one of four positions. On both sides, what is below the bar is the generally hidden component that must be present if the discourse effect of the top signifier is to be achieved. The terms used in each of the four locations are defined as follows: S1 is master signifier or symptom; S2 is knowledge; $ is the divided subject; and the *objet a* is a complex term that we can roughly think of as desire, but more precisely it is surplus *jouissance;* Samuels, in "Guest Editorial," defines it as "a letter or logical marker that marks the unknowability of the Other's desire and the real presence of existence and experience" (5). The S1 is also a complex term. S1, a master signifier, is not simply any example of discourse, but an element showing value; it embodies the ideals and most valued meanings of a culture or people.

These mathemes explain how recipients of discourse do not passively receive cultural meaning and value. To have a particular effect to a message, recipients must place themselves in relation to desire. In the discourse of the master, for example, followers are subjected to the power of the master's discourse only if they respond properly as desiring subjects. They must, in terms of the matheme, occupy the position of the Other at the top-right. To be in the Other position, however, means, in the case of master discourse, not simply to listen to a discourse but also to produce a desire (*objet a,* below the bar) as a response to the listening. Initially, then, this formula is simple. It suggests that people who follow other people believe because they want to believe. Lacan's formula, however, makes this simple observation very complex. It is not random pleasure that generates belief but a response to an authority that a person unconsciously wants. Psychoanalytic work on charisma and leadership offer useful contributions to understanding these relationships more fully.[7]

Master signifiers, the values held in place by the production of desire, are particularly important to the master's discourse; let me discuss them at some length. Master signifiers represent significations that are invested with desire. They are places at which subjects have attachments to ideas and feelings. They are most obviously terms that a subject identifies with. Mark Bracher, in *Lacan, Discourse, and Social Change,* explains that master signifiers are culturally defined and may be key terms such as *American, strong,* and *smart.* Master signifiers come to represent the subject. They "stand in" for subjectivity, filling in the lack of subjectivity with meaning and value. Of course, this meaning and value come from the master.

Kenneth Burke and Aristotle, like Lacan, understand persuasion as identification—the form of a production of desire to be like someone else. When speakers persuade us, we experience the same value in the signifiers they speak as they do. For example, if they speak positively about feminist issues, we will respond positively only if we identify with them. If we do not identify, we may understand what the speaker means, but we do not share the same views or values. This is because the act of identification (which depends on the unconscious gratification of desire) does not take place.

At the top of Lacan's matheme of master discourse are two signifiers, S1 and S2. In considering this topmost level, these signifiers suggest that master signifiers working as agents in discourse produce knowledge in the recipient. Postmodernists often claim, "Knowledge is ideological." This production of ideology, however, takes place only when the elements below the bar operate. Thus, S1 will function as a master signifier only when there is an $ or divided subject speaking *and* when this speech is recognized by a follower by a production of surplus desire, *objet a,* below the bar. Masters are masters when they have slaves, and slaves *will choose* to serve masters only if they want to.

In the discourse of the master, S1 works *as* knowledge or, S2, a chain of meaningful signifiers. S2 is the collection of meaningful representations belonging to a culture or a person. S2 is itself not truth but the collection of those things meaningful for a culture. S1 is part of S2 because it is meaningful, but it is different from S2 because it is valued. When what is valued by the master is accepted as an indisputable truth, the master's value assertion limits both the desires and the meanings that can circulate in a culture.

For example, a master signifier circulating as knowledge could be the signifier *England* when it becomes linked to a claim such as, "England is the greatest nation on Earth." In England, at a certain point in history, this claim would be received as obviously true. This truth, however, would be supported purely by subjects who had been subjected to the authority of culture (those subjects in the place of the Other). The political slogan passes as simple knowledge. But this false truth passes as truth, Lacan claims, because of the enjoyment given to those who repeat it. In addition, it restricts the production of other kinds of knowledge, such as the possible formula, "Germany is the greatest nation on Earth."

In the master's discourse, political slogans pass as knowledge because they are repeated. But these slogans are not repeated simply by means of force; the master's slogan is supported by the enjoyment found in those who, in receiving it, enjoy it, repeat it, and circulate it. We can see the effects of this phenomenon in classrooms whenever someone observes something with pleasure: "Did anyone else see *Ally McBeal* last night? It was great." Someone else might identify with something in this assertion, perhaps its hint at sophistication, and repeats the same observation with similar pleasure. If a third person then repeats the same observation, other people in the room, even if they did not see the show, may very well wish they had because it seems clear that the other people have something they do not, pleasure.

This pleasure, of course, is nothing material. But it is a real experience produced by a lack and by identification, and in this sense it has real presence. We can imagine, for example, a number of students looking forward to watching *Ally McBeal* for the first time and preparing to enjoy it. For Lacan, enjoyment is a response to what fills the lack of another significant other. This *filling* is an imaginary event, but it is a very real experience.[8]

Desire is an effect of a social relationship. We desire because the Other desires. Biological need will need to respond to something real, such as food, but desire does not. Joyful (even if unconscious) repetition is the force of ideological knowledge. The S_2 (really an ideological claim) received in the position of the Other is supported by the hidden *objet a*, surplus enjoyment, indicated below the bar on the graph. The graph reads that in the discourse of the master the production of the *objet a* supports the S_2, knowledge. Ideology, then, is supported by desire.

Ideological Power as Cultural Symptom

Once we grasp the spread of ideology as an effect of eager repetition, we can begin to understand how the desiring subject supports ideology. University discourse can train a subject to repeat an ideological truth, but it will not motivate a subject to want to repeat an ideological truth. Ideology, then, can circulate in a rote manner by university discourse, the simple memorization of signification. But ideology does not circulate effectively in this manner. To be effective, persuasive, and motivational, ideology needs to circulate as part of a master's discourse.

The matheme for master discourse also indicates that ideological knowledge is the effect not simply of desire and signification but of repression as well. The master signifier S1 is spoken by the agent as split subject. Masters are motivated to make a value assertion and circulate it in their followers as social truth precisely because they want to deny any possibility that they may not be a unified subject, in perfect control of their feelings, perceptions, and knowledge. In the Milgram experiment, for example, the command, "The experiment must continue," works to repress experiences of self-division. It banishes certain feelings for subjects divided between values, between loyalty to a victim who suffers and loyalty to an authority who commands suffering. In the experiment, this command was not fully articulated in relation to an ideological system, but it might easily have been so articulated. It could support the value of science when faced with those experiences that call the value of science into doubt. Students come to value science when they desire what the master desires.

Ellie Ragland observes that the "'master discourse' is arrogant because it assumes the master knows all there is to know" (72). Arrogance in the master is a form of defense. It defends against the master's incompleteness as a subject; it defends the master's own grandiosity against experiences of lack at an unconscious level.

The knowledge circulated by the master is supported by a repression of desires and fears, even as it supported in another sense by a circulation of the enjoyment embodied in the repetition of the master signifier. In *Tarrying with the Negative: Kant, Hegel, and the Critique of Ideology*, Slavoj Žižek points out that "the point of symbolic identification: the bond linking together [the] members [of a culture] always implies a shared relationship toward a Thing, toward Enjoyment incarnated" (201). If masters love the state as the *Thing*, it is the same as believing that England is the greatest nation on Earth. Masters can, in this manner, more easily deny their limitations and self-contradictions as people. Their master signifiers are their identities and symptoms, which they love more than themselves. In masters' love for their symptoms, they seek to form a community in which all subjects are recognized in terms of their love for the masters' symptoms. Subjects who do not share this love are threats to it.

The discourse of the master circulates the master's desire in social space, but as it functions, it also restricts desire. Only those desires given value by the master's symptom circulate. In the discourse of the master, enjoyment is found in repetition of ideology as *knowledge*. Knowledge, though, is a neurotic symptom, a defense against potential experiences of desire and intersubjective relations that reveal the master's lack of mastery.

David Metzger, in "Lacan and the Question of Rhetoric," points out that "symptoms . . . are a knot of signifiers that join our bodies to the satisfaction of the (death) drive" (18). Symptoms are fixated verbal and bodily expressions that imprison desire within obsessional and ultimately stultifying forms of repetition. In an ideal society, people would find plentiful satisfaction in happy discursive relations. Talk itself would offer stimulation and enjoyment as desire circulated freely in all forms of discourse. Because desire, in essence, can never be satisfied in any real object, it finds particular satisfaction in the unrepressed circulations of desire in speech and in the recognition experience it offers. When desires are fixated in symptoms, however, they do not find satisfaction in the play of discourse; they are threatened by free speech.

In suggesting that composition instruction can contribute to an anti-ideological identity, I seek to promote the composition class as a place to structure other possibilities for the circulation of desire. In ideal social relations, desire can be satisfied in conditions whereby the enjoyment of desire is itself challenged. Happy social relations are open to spontaneity and even conflict. In such situations, conflict does not stop the circulation of desire; it facilitates it. When a good friend tells us that our desire to see a popular movie, *Star War XXVII,* is stupid, for example, we listen with interest and prepare for an enjoyable conversation. In some conditions, an hour of talk about the movie might be more enjoyable than the movie itself. Such talk is enjoyable because it generates understanding, and understanding, more so than objects of demand, satisfies desire. Most social conditions, however, do not generate understanding but make conflict stressful. When an aloof authority tells us that our desire to see a popular movie is stupid, we are hurt, or silent and hostile, or vocal and hostile. Good dialectical conflict, as opposed to unproductive dialectical conflict, satisfies demand's need to find better, more suitable representations. Žižek explains:

> Demand almost always implies a certain dialectical mediation: we
> demand something, but what we are really aiming at through this de-
> mand is something else—sometimes even the very refusal of the demand
> in its literality. Along with every demand, a question necessarily rises:
> "I demand this, but what do I really want by it?" (22)

Žižek's emphasis on the importance of dialectical mediation suggests that most demands are for symbolic objects. There are, of course, real cases in which people need food and medical care, and demands for such material goods essential to life must be respected and carried forward by a political process. But in most of the Western world, demand most often seeks symbolic objects. Once people have enough food and shelter to live, they ask for status and the symbols of status: recognition or respect. Understanding gives recognition, and thus discourse can generate symbolic rewards. In theory, symbolic rewards can be generated through the circulations of desire in discourse.

While happy social discourse is dialectical, responsive to understandings that reformulate desire, the discourse of the master is characteristically nondialectical. It does not want to help people understand what they want; it wants people to find their enjoyment in the repetitive performances of the master's knowledge. Because desire can never be fully repressed, spontaneous and open relationships with others are threatening to the master, and relations to others are often controlled by use of polarized value terms taught by the master. Masters preside over social situations where there are good others and bad others. Bad others are enemies; their speech is evil and false; it threatens the social order. Good others are those who, like Orwell's citizens of *1984*, repeat Big Brother's slogans with happiness and conviction.

Masters provide imaginary solutions to problems of anxiety. Faced with danger, people generally feel that the presence of the leader gives security. Masters at times serve important needs. They unite people in acts of sacrifice and combat when real enemies present real threats. Masters, through the generation of master signifiers, provide reasons for sacrifices. Sacrifice considered thus becomes an idealized act of repression. Something desired is given up because something of higher value comes to seem more important. Masters thus make the act of sacrifice something that followers, in some sense, enjoy. But all cultures, while they may at times find masters useful, must also find ways to curb their power. Masters are always potentially dangerous. Their knowledge is always a neurotic knowledge based on repression.

As orators, masters have the power to justify the killing of another person by means of an appeal to a truth supported by a demand that cannot be compromised. Any demand, in principle, can be circulated by an effective master as one that cannot be compromised. Thus, a good follower of the far political right may echo a master who insists that abortions must end, and a good follower of the extreme political left may insist that research on animals must end. This list is, in theory, endless because masters are very creative in formulating projects that can give meaning and drama to the devotional sacrifices of their followers. The ultimate logic of the discourse of the master demands precisely that biological identity (and its relation to biological need) be sacrificed in the name of some signifier, the master signifier of the master's symptom.

We can say that masters fashion, or even generate, desire, but they do not circulate it effectively in relation to the full diversity of human desire. Robert Samuels, in a careful analysis of Lacan's *objet a*, argues that changes, both cultural and subjective, develop as we learn to recover our real experiences of desire that are "beyond the deadening effects of the signifier and the alienating results of the specular image" (5).

The recovery of emotional life from repression, the development of an anti-ideological identity as opposed to an ideological one, involves the use of the other discourse modes. Of those three discourses, the hysteric and analyst discourses are most effective in the circulation of desire. The speech of the hysteric responds to the master's lack with a demand for something more.

$$\frac{\text{\$}}{a} \quad \longrightarrow \quad \frac{S_1}{S_2}$$

In hysteric discourse, the *objet a* at the bottom-left supports the speech of a divided subject expressing its division. This leads to the production of the S_1 in its isolated form. The speech of the hysteric thus performs an important social function. It draws attention to the non-sense of the master. This non-sense gives pleasure to the follower of the master, but it does not satisfy the hysteric. The hysteric typically, unsatisfied by the explanations of the master, asks questions.

The master, threatened by the discourse of the hysteric, however, will seek ways to silence it. The speech of the hysteric will be placed in a context of reasoning (defensive ideological intellectualization) that demonstrates it to be bad, stupid, or nonsense. Because in most cultures the master defines most of what makes sense, the master's discourse, in most real social situations, has more power than that of the hysteric. It materializes sense. Yet this power can be undone by a mode of understanding that can represent what Žižek calls the *idiotic enjoyment* of the master's symptom. This kind of analysis, I would suggest, is something we can, and should, pursue in composition classes. At times, it is possible to expose the master's symptoms as pure idiocy. We might imagine that most of the changes in literary theory over the last twenty years have served this function. At first, it was necessary for everyone to submit to the master truth of the New Critics. Scholars, to publish, needed to show their seniors that they understood the real nature of literature. They needed to find ways to repeat the truths of New

Criticism. This truth, however, finally became subjected to questions that undermined its persuasive power. New masters and new truths developed, deconstructive, postmodernist and cultural. Psychoanalysis suggests that when truth becomes emptied of its imaginary idealization, it can be transformed into its opposite: shit. Thus, truth claims that unified scholars in happy discourse thirty years ago now generate repulsion and disgust.

In a democratic society, people make choices about their desires and the desires of others. Liberation thus requires that people understand their desires, that is, be educated about their desires. But this kind of education requires the free circulation of desire in speech, and it requires forms of dialectic that do not eliminate old masters only to set up new masters. It requires that all subjects freely speak their desires and that all subjects listen nondefensively, seeking to find where and how blockages in desire can be set free by more and better talk.

Beyond Binaries in the Analysis of Desire

Contemporary society requires the free circulation of desire, and composition classrooms should be privileged places where this circulation is practiced. What is necessary for the free circulation of desire is not simply happy energetic speech but the ability of a discourse community to express and listen to competing claims about desire, competing claims about what Slavoj Žižek calls, in *Tarrying With the Negative*, a particular group's "love for the Thing."

True freedom in the expression of desire involves developing skills in mediating between opposing desires found in a social field. Much like the resolution of the oedipal complex, freedom of expression of desire requires a triangulation of desire whereby a third person can find a place in relation to two important others. The Milgram experience suggests very clearly that humans have considerable difficulty responding to a social situation presenting two conflicting demands. Solutions to conflicts in demand are commonly found in acts of identification and defensive repression rather than in dialectical mediation. Dialectical mediation is always logically possible, but it is often not emotionally possible. In the case of the Milgram experiment, there was a context for legal and moral thinking that could have been evoked to work through a noncompliant but dialectical response to the demand made by the teacher. Most people, however, were not able to engage in this process of negotiation. The experiment continued by virtue of the teacher's simple demand, "The experiment must continue."

I have sought to describe negative restrictions in the free flow of desire in terms of the symptomatic nature of the master's discourse. Let me now provide an illustration of forms of discourse make use of triangulation and overcome symptomatic rigidity.

Lad Tobin, in a classic essay on countertransference in the classroom, describes a situation in which, confronted by hostile students, he learns to loosen his own fixation on demand, recover the ambivalence of his own feelings, and discover a way to generate discussion with students he dislikes. Tobin's essay suggests how difficult it can be for teachers to overcome a vast, silent, resentful gap that often separates students from teachers and undermines a teacher's ability to stimulate writing.

Tobin's essay is an important document for the psychology of the classroom, but I think it is important to read it as a metaphor for culture in general. Tobin describes one particular class, which he described as a "nightmare":

> I had trouble getting the students involved in the discussion or in their own writing, and I grew increasingly irritated during class. I was especially bothered by the four 18-year old male students who sat next to each other, leaning back in the desks against the wall. They usually wore sunglasses; they always wore sneakers with untied laces. Whenever I tried to create drama or intensity, they joked or smirked. Whenever I tried to joke, they acted aggressively bored, rolling their eyes or talking to each other. At first, I tried to ignore them, trying not to let them get to me. But I found that it was a little like trying not to think about an elephant. I was always aware of them, even when they were not acting out. (343)

Tobin's description of the lack of interaction between teacher and student indicates a clear lack of circulation of the simplest elements of socializing desire. Discussion and writing, Tobin notes, are difficult to initiate. The offending students are not only bored with what he says, they act repeatedly to deflate his ability to circulate desire as a teacher. They joke when he tries to be dramatic, and they roll their eyes when he tries to joke. It is clear here that discussion has become impossible because desire does not circulate in discourse from one person to another. Confrontation works precisely in terms of deflating desire. Rolled eyes kill the joke, intersubjective relations become impossible, and different expressions of desire are met with absolute opposition. Such interaction poisons discussion in the class and interferes with the writing that other students do.

Just as a classroom can be social site in which silence and thinly suppressed hostility separate people from one another, cultures also can be places in which intensely polarized differences hold in place an uneasy silence that separates people. Much politicized conflict can only be settled by a work of politics in which laws coerce people, whatever they make think or feel, into acting with more justice. But discourse, as a mechanism for shared feeling and intelligibility, must exist prior to any discourse of law and must also play a role in establishing law. An ideal society, like an ideal classroom, can generate discourse about difference as a play of meaning that is interesting rather than threatening and uncomfortable.

As someone who has been in the classroom for more than twenty-five years and has evaluated many classes of new instructors, I believe there is now less discussion in English classrooms than before. I think the reduction in talk is not a good thing, but it also seems that the apparently happy discussions we had earlier were not necessarily good either. Back in the 1970s, when most people ascribed to similar cultural ideals, it was easier for teachers to generate talk, but most of this talk simply circulated the desire of the master.

This happy talk of the 1970s did not often offer an effective critique of desire, but I do not think that the current demands for changes in desire are effective critiques either. Now, I think, there is less talk in the classroom, and part of the reason for that is because there is more confrontation with different student desires. Sometimes when I ask students about their unwillingness to talk, they say that everyone makes their own choices about their lives; they are religious or not, political or not, sexually active or not. All these choices are fairly intense forms of identification, and classroom talk does not seem able to open people up to recognize and respect other people with different identities. Talking can help in these situations, but one cannot simply start talking and expect things to get better. Students often feel as if there were nothing to say. Teachers may have a lot to say, but students often experience an uncomfortable silence.

Silence, and especially uncomfortable, sullen silence, is the most difficult position to start from for initiating talk. But from a Lacanian perspective, silence can be an especially useful place to start from if a discourse is to succeed in truly circulating desire in speech.

Silence signifies the place where there is hostility, where defenses operate, where desire can connect to no signifiers other than symptoms (political slogans), or where there is no place for intelligibility. Silence indicates a social context in which some of the meanings necessary for understanding are repressed. An ideal classroom, to me, would be one most sensitive at bringing speech out of silence and, conversely, able to lead speech into a kind of engaged, pregnant silence in which preconscious intuitions begin to materialize, even at the most primitive levels of signification, at a place where meaning had before been simply absent or irritating.

In most real social situations, desire is bound to particular signifiers.

Most of us, for example, belong to particular ethnic or cultural communities. Often this means that we are uncomfortable talking with people who do not value those things we have learned to value. In Tobin's example, there is a conflict between a cultural identity that values writing and one that does not. The more Tobin tries to solve the problem by talking more, the more he generates a more uncomfortable relationship. If dialogue were a simple answer to conflicts in cultural values, Tobin's initial verbal responses would cure the problem. But it doesn't. An effective circulation of desire requires something more skillful than energetic talk.

Tobin reports that when he became aware of his own anger and tried, as the authority in the situation, to reach beyond it, he developed a dialogical relationship with two students. Tobin's feelings had always been present in the situation, but they were also hidden. As he began to work with his feeling to change his relationship with his students, things improved. Two of the students began to write. The essays these students wrote as they responded to this new relationship speak their resistance and rebellion as students. But in speaking their rebellion, expressing their desires in communication, the students both circulate their desires and open their expression of desire as meanings that can meaningfully relate to a community. Tobin writes, "The fact that these challenges to my authority came in conventional forms that supported my authority neutralized my anger or defensiveness; the fact that I allowed and encouraged these challenges neutralized theirs" (345).

Tobin's example indicates how the circulation of desire is both difficult and important. If we examine the situation carefully, we may make better sense of the complex relations between freedom and social determination in the generation of discourse. Tobin's students are, in principle, always free to express themselves. But in truth, in Tobin's class, they are not free, initially, in any real sense. Their desires have been determined in many ways. They represent a culture that does not value what Tobin does. Tobin's presence and discourse present them with demands that makes expression impossible. The solution to this silence is not the assertion by an authority of some superior master signifier. When two subjects serving the demands of opposing masters confront each other, each insisting on conflicting demands, the result is not a change in subjectivity; the result is social conflict.

Lacan's discourses makes sense of how the common, unprofitable opposition between the dialogic ideal of humanist teaching and the diacritical model of the poststructuralist obscures crucial features in the circulation of desire. The free circulation of desire is not an easy state of social affairs. In *Tarrying with the Negative*, Žižek argues that "'subjectivization' . . . is a kind of defense mechanism against an abyss, a gap, which 'is' the subject" (171). What characteristically generates language in us is thus the workings of our defenses. Normal speech between two very different subjects, is thus normally a kind of war between opposing and mutually suspicious structures of defense. Each subject is a subject through the expression of a defense, and each subject has indefensible defenses to defend. As long as cultures were hegemonic, group discussion could be easy because it could exercise a variety of defenses that were often hostile to outsiders. Now that cultures are more heterogeneous, discussion is more difficult.

When we respond to others, (people different from ourselves who are speaking their desires) we are often unable to find ourselves in speech without giving offense. Sometimes, even when we try to be pleasant, we unconsciously express hostility. It is as if the conscious intention to be civil were overcome by an unconscious desire to find a scapegoat. In one episode of the PBS comedy, *Fawlty Towers,* the innkeeper Basil has guests from Germany. He emphatically tells his help that they absolutely must not make their visitors uncomfortable by talking about the war, but as soon as he greets his guests, he asks if they would like cocktails "before the war." The canned laughter in the background cranks up and Basil writhes in discomfort. He struggles to regain control, but as he seeks to talk more in order to put his guests at ease, more and more discomforting talk emerges. At one point, he utters, "Prisoners will be tied with piano wire," to his shocked guests who are waiting patiently to hear more about their hotel and its services. Probably this is an example not of everyday misdirection of speech but of humorous exaggeration. We laugh because we ourselves never make such mistakes, but we laugh as well because we recognize how such Freudian slips are made.

Culturally diverse human communities face particular challenges because people are not free to express themselves in speech. We can understand this situation as similar to Žižek's description of patriots confronting their identities in the gaze of people different from themselves. In such a situation, we see our identity as our *Thing:*

> Something accessible only to us, as something "they" the others, cannot grasp; nonetheless it is something constantly menaced by "them." It appears as what gives plenitude and vivacity to our life, and yet the only way we can determine it is by resorting to different versions of the same empty tautology. (*Tarrying* 201)

Desire does not circulate freely simply by means of dialogue, as humanists might insist, because subjectivity is, in essence, a defense structure. Spontaneous expressions of speech typically generate defensive expressions, and social fields populated by diverse cultural identities experience tension. Now, as culture becomes increasingly heterogeneous, there is a need to make discourse work, but current cultural conditions also make it harder for discourse to work.

Social-constructionists might insist that freedom is irrelevant and that politically progressive teachers should simply assert their values as those that the students must adopt. But this solution will not work either. We may *demand* change of others or even in ourselves, but such demands are only another form of fixation. Desires, once again, become fixated and defensive, generating enemies where there is only difference. Tobin works better as a teacher when he frees himself from the repressive immobility of his anger, finding ground for his own desire in relation to the desires of his students.

Important changes in subjectivity can take place in the field of social discourse only when desire begins to circulate in social space as open and dialectically responsive to the desires acknowledged in the discourse of others. If we ask how the dialectic of desire in Tobin's class begins to change, we might answer in two ways. Tobin, as a teacher makes, we might say, a free act to change how he expresses his demand. Tobin, by a free act of thought, discovers that his anger and his anxious insistence are not helpful. This sentence suggests that Tobin is a free agent. Another answer would be to suggest that Tobin, as a teacher trained in psychoanalytic relations, is led to find a solution to his classroom problem by reference to the theoretical ideas that define his scholarly identity. The material conditions of the classroom drive Tobin to seek a solution, and the theoretical ideas that define his thinking offer a solution. This sentence suggests that Tobin is an effect of discourse. It seems to me that the two theoretical answers are not so different. Both answers draw attention to the important relation between discourse and desire. This present book is an attempt to emphasize the importance of Tobin's act as a teacher and an attempt to materially rephrase, emphasize, and circulate the discourse context that makes his act possible.

The Circulation of Desire in the Discourses

Having focused on the discourse of the master and the problems it presents, I turn to Lacan's other three discourses to describe how the circulation of desire becomes possible when the four different discourses are able to freely shift, interact, and mutually influence each other. I begin with a historical approach and end with a concrete example from personal experience.

As recently as three hundred years ago, most truth claims were easily supported by the mere insistence of important people. Kings claimed that they ruled by divine right; clerical leaders claimed to know the will of God and exterminated anyone foolish enough to disagree; many Catholic priests claimed it was God's plan to exterminate Protestants; and many Protestant clergymen claimed it was God's plan to exterminate Catholics. Strong leaders made clear truth claims, and followers were willing to sacrifice their lives in their demonstrations of allegiance.

If truth claims supported by a sheer act of allegiance to a leader are no longer popular and, in fact, are common examples of sheer idiocy, it is due, in part, to the influence of a secular, impartial, rational discourse. This discourse, one that demands a detached and objective manipulation of signification, is Lacan's discourse of the university.

Many theorists suggest that the modern world is most characterized not by the discourse of the master but by the discourse of the university. After the Enlightenment, the rise of science, and all the work done in the West on authoritarian personalities, masters are not as popular as they once were. The discourse of the university, some now argue, offers the solution to the discourse abuses of the master. In the discourse of the university, it might seem, all desires and all knowledges circulate freely.

In contrast to the discourse of the master, the discourse of the university does not seek to produce knowledge defined by enjoyment; it simply reproduces knowledge as signification. On the top-left side of the matheme that represents the discourse of the university is S_2, knowledge, in the place of the agent.

$$\frac{S_2}{S_1} \rightarrow \frac{a}{\$}$$

In the discourse of the university, the four elements rotate one step to the left. S_1 was above the bar in the discourse of the master; it is below the bar in the discourse of the university. At the top-left side, the place where discourse is received, is the *objet a*. We read this formula as suggesting that, in the discourse of the university, knowledge is received when students repress their self-division and present themselves as desiring only the S_2 offered by the teacher.

Although the *objet a*, the object cause of desire, is above the bar in the discourse of the university, it would be wrong to see the discourse of the university as one that makes desire visible. Enjoyment, in university discourse, does not connect to real subjects at all. The $\$$ below the bar suggests that in university discourse truth has no relation to subjectivity. In this discourse there is no place for desire except in the desire to contain knowledge.

In this way, the discourse of the university paradoxically involves a suppression of desire more dramatic than that demanded by the master. This suppression creates a condition whereby subjects have no relation whatsoever to their own desire. I should point out that this suppression is not always bad; it has a positive feature. The discourse of the university provides a space in which knowledge can be produced even if certain feelings within the subject oppose the knowledge taught.

In the discourse of the university, the reception of knowledge works precisely through the suppression of individualized feeling or desire. In this discourse, the subject says "the facts compel me," "logic compels me," or, "the rules require the following." There may even be a masochistic enjoyment with this statement; a lack in the subject is filled in by this knowledge. But the subjects' relation to their own desired, their truths as divided subjects, is under the bar, in repression. The discourse of the university provides an enormously useful function as it can effectively counter the discourse of the master. Truth in university discourse is never a direct effect of someone's personal experience or insistence but an effect of the facts, evidence, or logic. In the discourse of the master, the *desire* to believe something counts as *evidence* for truth. In the discourse of the university, the desire to believe that something is true will never *consciously* count as evidence that something is true. Indeed, such use of evidence is against the rules of the university.

In the discourse of the university, knowledge can be received in an apparently objective fashion precisely because it functions in a position apart from subjectivity. Unlike the discourse of the master, that of the university does not require the subject to enjoy the idiotic truth of some master signifier. Students need only memorize the facts, or act as if the facts matter, not the experience of the subject.

The discourse of the university might be partly understood in terms of the old joke about university teaching: It is a process whereby information moves from the notes of the professor to the notes of the student without passing through the minds of either. Here, truth does not function through the production of a largely repressed experience of identification and enjoyment. Instead, truth is empty of experience; it is produced through the laws of a representational discursive system that acts as if subjectivity and experience were irrelevant. The body of the subject serves simply as a notational device for the inscription of signification.

Many, if not all, styles of teaching employ the discourse of the university.

Education requires that subjects flatten their personal desires in order to receive knowledge. Lacan's argument, however, is that desire is not eliminated, but it merely shifts. The students' desire is expressed only as a desire to learn. What is learned has no relation to the personal experience of subjectivity. If we say that there are objective rules of writing that students must learn, if we say that there are facts that students must know, we speak the discourse of the university.

The discourse of the university has important social uses. In the 1960s, when I was growing up in the South, most students wanted to believe that slaveholders were kind and benevolent people. The last decade of scholarship in African-American Studies has shown such a belief to be nothing more than wishful defensive thinking. This scholarship has been effective in asserting that despite what some people might want to believe, the facts are otherwise.

The discourse of the university, while it has its uses, also has problems. Lacan's formula shows that S2, spoken by the university spokesperson, is supported by the hidden truth of an S1, a master signifier. This suggests that most objective scholars, whatever they may claim, unconsciously serve generally invisible masters. Most scholars live in an academic world complicated by many truth claims, but most scholars find one theory right and another wrong. Scholars insist, much like kings claiming divine right, that their truth is true and that of another is false. And so, as Foucault insists, one must always seek to uncover not only what is true but also who benefits from a particular truth claim.

Lacan's theory of desire would suggest that people are enormously shaped and determined by the desire of the master and disciplined by the knowledge produced by the university. When these two discourses operate to reinforce each other, as they often do, they very effectively determine what people think and how they act, feel, and behave. We can imagine, for example, people living in particular religious, political, or professional communities in which they serve powerful masters in various ways but at the same time identify with a system they imagine as a logical university discourse. They are many times when this rational discourse conflicts with the demands made by a particular master, but most people find ways to survive these conflicts and to use their rationality to support the truth claims of their masters. But if I say this, I should also say that good teachers often find ways to use university discourse to undo such attachments. Such shifts in allegiance are never easy, but many teachers develop skill at effecting certain kinds of shifts by making certain conflicts visible and resolvable. I believe Berlin's ideal for teaching, in making visible and resolving conflict, is very much possible, but it is not a simple function of debate. This making visible of the repressed involves the discourses of the analyst and of the hysteric. Before I discuss the discourse of the analyst in depth, I need to make the intermediate step to show how conflict can be, and needs to be, elaborated by another discourse form, the discourse of the hysteric.

The discourse of the master and the discourse of the university comprise the largest visible component of social discourse. Nonetheless, these two discourses are never totally successful in creating subjects in total submission to masters and universities. Lacan argues that every subjectivity is grounded in lack and thus some aspect of every subject's desire is not determined by the social system. Dylan Evans explains that in the seminars of 1962–63, Lacan began to define the *objet a* as "the leftover, the remainder (Fr. Reste) of the symbolic in the real" (125). Later, as he developed his theory of the four discourses, Lacan suggested that, "In the discourse of the master one signifier attempts to represent the subject for all other signifiers, but inevitably a surplus is always produced; this surplus is *objet petit a*, a surplus meaning, and a surplus enjoyment" (125). This remnant of desire, this empty space within subjective meaning is the place where meaning forms. It is like the empty space in those small plastic games in which one moves a sequence of numbers around on a flat grid. One can work through all the possible permutations of relationship among numbers to get them into a correct sequence, but the numbers can be moved about only because there is an empty space where they can move.

Humans also can move about different desires, different desires for different objects. New significations can take on meaning, and new relationships can bring meaning into visibility. Ideally, human desire is metonymic; it can entertain all possible meanings. This is true because nothing essential to subjectivity anchors human meaning.

This basic lack that is the ground of desire is not free; it is always filled in by various accidents of signification. Nonetheless, this piece of desire conflicts with a social system that seeks to proscribe and limit desire. Thus, some component of every person's identity will find satisfaction in some fragment of desire operating counter to social demand. Subjects will discover food preferences, truth preferences, sexual preferences, consumer preferences, or preferences in the nature of social experience that are in conflict with forms of desire demanded by masters.

When subjects speak their own desire in opposition to the discourses of the master or the university, they most frequently speak the discourse of the hysteric. Hysterical subjects are in touch with basic lack. They are those subjects always not fully satisfied by the manner in which desire is generated by the master or suppressed by the university. The hysterical subject complains, challenges, and/or confronts the discourses of the master or university. The matheme for the hysteric is:

$$\frac{\$}{a} \longrightarrow \frac{S_1}{S_2} \qquad \text{hysteric discourse}$$

Compared to the matheme for the master, the matheme for the hysteric shows all elements moving one step to the right from the master discourse. Reading the top of the matheme we see that the divided subject speaks directly. This places, in the position of the Other, not S_2, knowledge, but S_1, a particular subject's statement of its unique mode of enjoyment whereby S_2 is under repression.

Hysterical subjects perform an important social function. They oppose the forms of social control of desire utilized effectively by the master and by the university. Victor Vitanza, in "An Open Letter to My 'Colligs,'" argues that hysterical discourse must be given greater recognition. Indeed, the circulation of the hysteric's discourse is crucial for the circulation of desire in discourse. In the face of the master's demand, the hysteric asks a question. In the face of the university's assertion, the hysteric asks a question. While other subjects find fullness in the speech of the master or the university, the hysteric experiences emptiness.

Both masters and universities can find use for tactful questions. But in principle, the full force of questions undermines the power of both the master and the university. Questions that are allowed to proliferate without limit, like those of Hamlet seeking a final reason for existence, ultimately find no answer. Thus, the hysteric can both enrich various systems of meaning and threaten them.

If the discourse of the university is able to undermine the discourse of the master, the discourse of the hysteric is able to undermine the discourse of the university. The discourse of the hysteric performs an enormously important social function: It reveals the lack in other discourses. But like the other discourses, the discourse of the hysteric also poses problems. One problem in making use of the hysteric's discourse is that of making sense of it. Because hysterical subjects are not recognized as subjects in the terms offered by the discourse of the master or the university, their speech often does not make sense. The discourse of the hysteric does not initially fit in relation to other discourse. The matheme shows that the S_2, knowledge, the linking of signifier to signifier in a manner that makes sense, is hidden under the bar. Nonetheless, in the face of such opposition, hysterical subjects protest. They are able to act in that way because they respond to the social field in terms of their unique mode of experiencing desire. In *Lacanian Theory of Discourse*, Mark Bracher explains:

> The hysterical structure is in force whenever a discourse is dominated
> by the speaker's symptom—that is, his or her unique mode of experi-
> encing *jouissance*, a uniqueness that is manifested as a failure of the sub-
> ject . . . to coincide with or be satisfied by the master signifiers offered
> by society. . . . (122)

The hysteric protests the oppressive functioning of the master and the university. Because such protest is a symptom, though, it often does not connect well to other discourses. Hysterical discourse then does not usu- ally circulate effectively in the social field. To the extent that the protest is uniquely symptomatic, it will not connect to a larger field of discourse that operates in any social body as *understanding*. Thus, the discourse of the hysteric is very useful in standing up to the demands of an oppressive mas- ter, but to be effective it requires a work of linking and translation.

The last, discourse, that of the analyst, is the only discourse (according to Lacan) that can give an answer to the speech of the hysteric and pro- duce knowledge of desire. In this discourse, the person acting as analyst (who need not be an analyst) offers subjects a reading of their own signi- fiers of desire, at a moment when they are present in the subject's own dis- course but not in the subject's conscious mind. The matheme for the dis- course of the analyst is:

$$\frac{a}{S_2} \longrightarrow \frac{\$}{S_1}$$

In this discourse, both desire and the divided subject are above the bar of repression. In this moment of insight of desire, subjects discover their own desire as a meaning that has relations to a wider world of signification. This recognition of desire acting in the place of the subject is often equated with the meaning of the psychoanalytic cure. Patients, at the end, know their own desires. But this representation of the end of analysis in the rec- ognition of desire is clearly an oversimplification of numerous paradoxes that attend any meaning of what might be termed *desire, subjectivity*, and *an end*.

The recognition of desire that comes at the end cannot be the recogni- tion of any particular thing that defines desire; Lacan is clear that desire is most essentially a lack that cannot be filled except by a signifier that has no signified, no object in the real world. If the end of analysis recognizes desire but recognizes that no particular desire is *it*, the Thing, what is this end that can never really be an end? Part of what is clear here is that new recognitions of desire also involve new recognitions of what is not desired. That is to say, symbolic objects that have been fixated as objects of desire are given up.

Therapy in this way offers a discipline for developing new, less defensive modes of being in discourse. The analysand discovers new modes of relating to desires that are in discourse, and this means relating to other people and their desires with a lower level of defense.

Some of Lacan's work suggests that what is recognized about desire is precisely the discursive nature of desire. One does not recognize desire and thereby get it. One instead recognizes that "self" and others have desire. To be in discourse is to be in relation to multiple competing desires. This new form of being in relation means that one can consciously respond to the desires of others rather than have one's unconscious desire act as an automatic mechanism of defense.

Stasis Theory, Cultural Debate, and the Four Discourses

I suggested earlier that Lacan's theory of the four discourses in many ways resembles Jim Kinneavy's theory of four discourses. Persuasive discourse is similar to the discourse of the master. Informative discourse is the discourse of the university. Lacan's theory suggests that we see discourses in their relations to desire and repression. In informative discourse, like university discourse, desire is suppressed; in persuasive discourse, like the master's discourse, desire is produced. Lacan's account of the discourse of the hysteric and the discourse of the analyst are largely compatible with Kinneavy's accounts of literary and expressive discourse. In expressive or hysteric discourse, Lacan and Kinneavy would agree that individual desire is expressed. In Lacan's account, hysteric discourse is unique to self-expression; self-understanding, however, would never be a simple effect of self-expression. Because the self is fundamentally divided, it must rely on the other discourses for understanding.

Kinneavy bases his four-discourse theory on the communication triangle, and in an interesting but perhaps not fully convincing manner he argues that the discourse that represents the medium of discourse itself, discourse as code, is literature. Lacan might link discourse codes to the discourse of the analyst. His theory of the discourse argues that the unconscious is discovered as a code.

By suggesting that we think about discourse in relation to desire, Lacanian theory encourages us to consider new ways of thinking about the human interactions that produce discourse. If we think of the hysteric's question as a basic mechanism for the circulation of desire in culture, we

can develop better models for understanding how argumentation and dialectic can work in the classroom.

Many teachers, for example, teach argumentation and persuasion in relation to stasis theory. Stasis theory looks at argumentation in terms of
how people work to ask and answer questions. Different representations of
stasis theory formulate different wordings for the different types of questions asked, but there is general agreement on four general claims that generate and respond to argument. These four claims become questions that
must be answered by argument: questions of fact and definition, "What is
it?"; questions of value, "Is it any good?"; questions regarding cause and
effect, "How did it get this way?"; and proposals, "Let us do this." These
categories do not perfectly reflect Lacanian categories, but two categories
give useful insight into the Lacanian discourses as they circulate in a social field. Proposals, when they are formulated as demands, are the discourse of the master. A demand is made that something be done. Statements of fact and definition are the discourse of the university as are,
perhaps, cause-and-effect claims. Statements of value might function as a
master discourse as well.

Stasis theory argues that proposals involve all the different kinds of inquiry working in relation to each other. For example, if someone proposes
to build a bridge, people may be motivated to ask, "Why do we need a
bridge? Where would the bridge be placed? What kind of bridge would be
built? Do the benefits of having a bridge outweigh the expense and bother
of building one?" Proposals generate a wide array of questions when a social group allows questions to complicate the understanding required to allow a proposal to reach consensus.

If we pushed this simple example a bit further, we might say that the
health of any society depends on its ability to make sense of its desire in
relation to a demand. This means, necessarily, that many questions must
be asked and answered. This process of asking questions and finding answers does not take place automatically. In some communities, people in
authority simply tell others what they must do. Communities that more effectively satisfy desire, however, generate a diversity of questions and answers.

Going back to Amartya Sen's claim that famines have not taken place in
democratic societies, we can imagine how the play of discourse, generated
by hysteric and master discourse, and operating much like the introduction of a proposal, works to deliver needed goods to needy people. As a Peace
Corps volunteer during the near-famine in 1972, in Bidar District, Mysore
State, India, I could see very early on that the season's usual harvest would

not be forthcoming. The plants that most needed water for survival were the first to dry up, and villagers began to plan how they might cope with what they knew would be a difficult year. When the sorghum withered in the field, villagers began to horde foodstuff, and merchants were accused of raising prices on rice. There was a clear sense of emergency in all the rural villages, and it was important that news about local conditions reach the state capital quickly. When local papers began to run stories on the severity of the drought, state newspapers ran stories on an impending calamity and there was a great call on the government for help. When the village wells slowly dried up, the village began to shift to a crisis state. As the representation of crisis reached high proportions, state and local governments proposed various means of relief. Many families walked long distances in the early morning to villages that still had drinking water. There were rumors that some poorer families chose between those children they would feed and those they would drown. State officials sought to alleviate the problem by delivering supplies. Drinking water and rice were brought in by trucks. In one local village, sacks of rice intended for famine relief were delivered to a village headman's warehouse in secret by night. News of this action spread, however, and even though this man had his *goondas* guarding the warehouse, a large number of lower-caste farmers went to the place and demanded the foodstuff the government had sought to deliver. This headman, fearful of violence and lacking political support, gave up the rice he had illegally hoarded. In this situation, large-scale death by starvation was averted by both a flow of information and a political climate that refused to accept starvation as an inevitable natural event. Village headmen, who in earlier times simply imposed their will on the lower castes, found themselves held accountable for the larger public good. At the most raw political moment, starving lower-caste villagers made demands, threatened violence, and got their food. But the success of this demand should not imply that demands are the only means of political progress. Demands for food, in this case, work because responses to desires have already triggered a network of social relations that deliver food to the needy. Farmers wanted to talk about their condition before they actually confronted starvation; reporters wanted to write about impending disaster; civil servants wanted to solve social problems; and Indian intellectuals sought to write new laws governing caste relations.

The circulation of desire by discourse is not the work of any one discourse. All discourse types play a role. In *Encore*, Lacan argued "there is some emergence of psychoanalytic discourse whenever there is a movement from one discourse to another" (16). I take this to mean that whenever we experience a shift in discourse as meaningful, whenever this movement gives us something we want in some sense, we respond to a shift in desire.

This experience of the question as a meaningful event need not, however, take place. When the demand of a master, for example, is met with an hysterical question, people can simply feel that the question is an impertinence or an insult. As an agricultural adviser in India, part of my job was to bicycle to various small villages, gather farmers together, and dispense information about crop fertilization and protection. In most of the villages I visited, I would first greet the traditional headman who would gather the farmers for my talk. It was a stock phrase for headmen to begin their speeches with words I still remember after thirty years, *Nanu heltini; Niu kelri* (I am speaking; you listen). This phrase introduced a moment when a headman wanted to make a formal statement to his village. There was a marked change in discourse style, and villagers usually moved to a sitting position around the headman. The headman spoke. Interruptions were not tolerated; the few questions that emerged later were greeted with an expression of contempt or disdain that was (oddly to my mind then) found particularly worthy of admiration by most of those who were sitting. The manufacturing of consent was not a complicated process in the first village where I lived, but it was a more difficult process in my second village, where different factions were able to compete for political power. In this village, political gatherings were lively and confrontational, and a wider range of villagers had a voice in local affairs.

We all know that asking questions and responding to them are important exercises necessary for democratic processes. Often, however, we do not realize that questions emerge only when people experience a desire to ask a question and feel the freedom to be able to act on that desire. Furthermore, expressed questions have an effect on a social body only where there is context that provides space for the question to shift desire into different discursive directions. This shift, importantly, will not occur when the master has the power to silence an expressed question with a simple repetition of his demand (as when Milgram's teacher says, "The experiment must continue").

Modern American culture has mixed feelings about questions. Sometimes they are seen as irritating interruptions; at times, though, they are very much valued. If a question is experienced as important, then I think we can say that a Lacanian shift from one discourse type to another has occurred. The discourse of the master has been loosened by the discourse of the hysteric. The question has introduced a space for the emergence of desire; it suggests that there is more to life than the simple, literal, fulfillment of the master's demand. These shifts can take place with relative ease when we develop cultures that allow people to speak their minds freely. If the freedom to speak goes back under repression (as in some communities), the shifts in discourse necessary for the health of a community may not take place easily or at all.

Though members of democratic societies pride themselves on their freedom of speech, I find that the generation of truly dialectical discourse, one fully open to questions, is a very difficult task for most of my students.[9] When I assign proposal papers to students, the best writers anticipate the desires and questions of their audience. These students have internalized in their own minds the subjective responses of others. They have heard many of these responses, and they can imagine what other people might say when presented with new ideas. Most people, however, have difficulty thinking of questions that other people might have about what they think. Sometimes they are very talkative about their own ideas, but when I tactfully try to ask questions, they will fall silent. Students tend to live their habitual ways of looking at situations as the only way. When they are prompted to be dialectical, it takes them time to generate thought. Sometimes, they know very well that there are other ways of looking at things, but they have difficulty thinking what these other viewpoints might possibly be.

5 Engaging Affect
Dialectic, Drive, and the Mourning of Identity

Thus far, I have examined two prominent postmodernist approaches to changing students, the analytic and argumentative approach of Berlin and the demand-of-knowledge approach of Ebert. In this chapter, I review one more common postmodernist model for changing subjectivity. Richard Rorty, in "Feminism and Pragmatism," provides a striking example of a certain popular, optimistic, and postmodernist view of language when he supports Katherine MacKinnon's feminist political project for simply extending the meanings of everyday words. In one essay, Rorty supports MacKinnon's plan in *Feminism Unmodified* to change male attitudes toward rape. This change requires, Rorty observes, that people feel "revulsion and rage where they once felt indifference or resignation" (43). Clearly, what must be generated here is a new emotional response. Rorty argues this new response can be produced by language that provides an *extension of logical space*. If social injustice is perpetuated by thoughtless and unreflective habits of thought, and if social justice is impeded by a acceptance or indifference to such habits of injustice, new language, producing new logical space and emotional response, can lead people to no longer tolerate what they once unthinkingly accepted. Rorty explains:

> One way to change instinctive emotional reactions is to provide new language that will facilitate new reactions. By "new language" I mean not just new words but also creative misuses of language—familiar words used in ways that initially sound crazy. Something traditionally regarded as a moral abomination can become an object of general satisfaction, or conversely, as a result of the increased popularity of an alternative description of what is happening. Such popularity extends logical space by making descriptions of situations that used to seem crazy seem sane. (43)

If Berlin invites his students to argue and Ebert demands from her students the recognition of certain truths, Rorty makes the least demand on students. He simply invites them to imagine the world differently. Rorty's goals are ambitious, to "change instinctive emotional reactions," and his plan for this change is to adopt "creative misuses of language."

Instinctive emotional reactions normally imply spontaneous emotive impulses that precede language use. Rorty's argument, however, invites us to consider a different relation: changes in language can change instinctive response. Rorty's hope that logical space can be extended by creative misuses of language reflects new assumptions about the nature of language and subjectivity. Because reality is at least in part constructed by language and because subjects (and their instinctive responses) are interpellated, or brought into existence by discourse, new discourse performances are imagined as effective mechanisms for the formulation of new modes of subjectivity and social reality. These new uses of language, it is argued, will produce new instinctive responses. Throughout this book, I argue that the subject's involvement with desire in language is key to changing the subject's involvement with ideology. Rorty's appeal to creative misuses of language might well work as an appeal to desire and, thus, promise the kind of change I myself advocate.

To show the limitations of Rorty's position, I need to return to the argument I made in the second chapter regarding the subject's pathological attachment to forms of subjectivity that cause suffering. In this chapter, I expand on that argument, suggesting that there are two forms of attachment that limit the dialectical developments of language.

In the previous chapter, I used Lacanian theory to outline the development of a discursive dialectic that moves from a discourse of a master to various discourses—that of the university, the hysteric, and the analyst—that keep acts of understanding mobile, fluid, and constantly adaptive. Composition courses often work precisely in terms of the discursive developments these shifts in discursive positions offer. When textbooks suggest, for example, that students develop their papers by asking questions, researching, and quoting authorities, they make appeals to the use of hysteric, university, and master discourses.

Teachers frequently want us to imagine this developmental process as a natural and essentially happy one. Textbooks often offer students a series of questions that should be heuristic, that should initiate the eager generation of thought. This kind of dialectical development is often imagined as tapping into the mind's own spontaneous generation of thought. Janet Emig, in "Writing as a Mode of Learning," describes the "talk" that precedes writing as "rich, luxuriant, inherently redundant" (87). Teaching and textbooks frequently ask us to imagine the dialectical process as one in which learning is effortless and pleasant, without sullen or confrontational resistance.

This ideal of a fully mobile and fluid movement of speech, questions, and understanding, however pleasant it is as a fantasy, is a fantasy. Lacan's theory of the four discourses might seem to suggest that the shifts in desire necessary for the production of new speech and discourse are effortless. But psychoanalysis itself is a process preoccupied with the analysand's resistance to new speech and understanding. This, indeed, is the same problem that is receiving more and more attention in composition theory. In chapter 3, I quoted from Richard's Boyd's, "Reading Student Resistance: The Case of the Missing Other":

> With the emergence of the student-centered classroom and the influence of expressivist rhetoricians like Peter Elbow and Donald Murray, it was to be expected that the old narratives of instructor and students locked in a struggle of wills would be replaced by a new version of a far more peaceable classroom where teachers might act more as collaborators than as adversaries. (590)

When composition theory gave up a paradigm of writing "correctness," it hoped that writing would automatically become more meaningful, productive, and easy. Such a dream of happy productive discourse did not, as Boyd notes with bitterness, materialize:

> My experience and my readings of these various [contemporary] narratives of student resistance suggest that we are not yet at that place where liberatory pedagogy can move on to other issues, confident that at least this one legacy of the current-traditional rhetoric need no longer be a consuming obsession of the discipline. (592)

Those of us who teach writing want to believe that learning to write is a pleasurable event, and often it is. But it is a mistake to believe that writing (and the political advances it can effect) is essentially pleasant. Writing is always haunted by masters and interlaced with forms of authority or correctness that we cannot easily abandon without guilt or discomfort.

All real subjects, as I suggested earlier, are subjects of defense. The ego, as a field of self-consciousness, is a defensive structure. This means that people have irrational forms of attachment that arrest the dialectical movement of discourse across the four discourses. These irrational attachments mean that even the inner speech that precedes writing is not rich and luxuriant. Often, when teachers gain energy in their own speech, students fall strangely silent. They are at a loss for words; they are sometimes confused, uncomfortable, or silent. Often this silence masks a pain that will not, or cannot, be spoken.

In this chapter, I explore two forms of attachment that typically limit, or in some cases completely prohibit, dialectical development. We begin to understand student resistance when we understand the attachments that are causes for the cessation of inner speech. Rorty's dream of inventive uses of language would work if subjectivity were not defined by various forms of libidinal attachment. One form of attachment, I suggest, cannot be undone; it is pathologically fixed and even psychotherapy is not likely to prove effective in achieving change. Another form of attachment, which I describe as a *mourning effect,* shows clear evidence of fixation, but these fixations can be loosened over time. Humans do, indeed, as postmodernist theory claims, have considerable plasticity in relation to discourse. But all subjects have some attachments that are not plastic, and some have enormously rigid and immovable forms of attachment that I, following the work of Slavoj Žižek, term *drive-fixated demands.*

We have all been in arguments in which our opponents were not led to new emotions by the happy and creative use of language that Rorty advocates. Such rigidity of political and moral belief is generally recognized. We have all been in arguments in which we may even have had enough evidence to support our claims, great clarity in our development, and creative uses of language, yet we failed to move our interlocutor. We reach a point at which we encounter either simple denial and/or an illogical counterattack.

When we encounter resistance like this, we meet points of libidinal attachment that cannot be moved by discourse. John Clifford emphasizes that prior social relations are an important dimension of resistances of this sort:

> the illusion . . . that we can somehow change the minds of others in
> a rhetorical vacuum freed from the pollutants of prior social align-
> ments . . . denies identity, represses class conflict, negates the way ideas
> originate in specific social configurations. (44)

Clifford's target for attack in this quote is a St. Martin's text on composition. Clifford's argument is not in response to Rorty's hope for the production of new emotions by language but the general liberal commitment to fair and rational argument. Such a belief, Clifford says, "asks writers to believe that by adopting and carefully orchestrating an objective, rational argument, they can win the day and bring Jesse Helms to his senses" (44). Clifford's critique of rational argument, however, is equally true for Rorty's dream of creative language. Just as Jesse Helms is not likely to be changed or influenced by good rational argument, they are not likely to be led by creative uses of language to new instinctive emotions. This is true because, at the level of prior social alignments and social configurations, Helms is

rigidly fixed in discourse by ideological and psychological forces that cannot be easily undone by appeals to new emotions, determined and reasonable attempts at discussion, or demands of authorities seeking to impose
their mastery on others.

Žižek invites us to understand Helms's lack of reason and unresponsive-
ness to creative uses of language as a pathological attachment. What this
means, in part, is that an aspect of his identity is caught in a fixed position,
caught in a structure of desire that sustains him as a subject. He cannot
imagine giving up this position because such a loss would be tantamount
to ceasing absolutely to be.

We all want to believe that discourse can play a role in social change
but, given this fixed position of the subject in language and fantasy, how
can this happen? How can discourse stimulate social change? How can discourse unravel the instinctive libidinal texture of social alignments that
hold subjects in particular positions of identity?

Contemporary theories of discourse sometimes imply that if we can just
control talk, we can control political belief. Such an assumption is naive.
Talk is not effective simply because it fills the air or books; it is effective
when it works on the desires that trigger particular meaning effects. This
is not to say that the materiality and authority of books are unimportant
for political effects; it is simply to insist that such materiality and authority
will be effective only when they actually have a real effect on the experiences and feelings, conscious and unconscious, of a real person.

How can discourse extend logical space? How does discourse construct
or change subjects by extending fantasy space? How does discourse undo
very emotional prior attachments that people instinctively have to their
own ideas and identities? Poststructuralist thought is not able to give satis-
factory answers to these questions without making use of psychoanalytic
concepts.

How Subjectivity Is Not Structured by Discourse

Most poststructuralist models of subjectivity describe subjectivity as an
essentially linguistic structure. In this sense, poststructuralism follows a
model that has been developed with particular clarity by the Marxist phi-
losopher Louis Althusser. For Althusser, as I discussed in chapter 1, subjects become subjects by being introduced to discourse. This theory of subjectivity has implications for teaching. In *Problémes Etudiants*, Althusser
emphasized teaching as a mode of introducing knowledge from a subject
who knows to a subject who does not know. "The function of teaching is to
transmit a determinate knowledge to a subject who does not possess this
knowledge" (154). Change in subjectivity would function here, much as it

does with Rorty, according to a metaphor of discourse addition. More discourse is added to a subject and the subject, with its instincts, changes.

Lacan's work indicates that the introduction of a new discourse will effect a change only if the subject's desire can make use of this discourse. Real change requires not the discursive production of new knowledge [as discourse] but a certain mobility in desire, a shift in the *objet a*. While a block of language can be transferred from one subject to another subject, the *objet a* that determines the meaning effects of this block of language cannot be so transferred. A teacher can force subjects to repeat signifiers that might seem to embody a progressive understanding of social relations, but there is no assurance that students will be interpellated as subjects by these meanings.

This is true because some kernels of subjectivity are isolated from the effects of intersubjective speech. They are not meanings open to intersubjective discussion, to an exchange or interaction of rational thought or mediating fantasy. An essential kernel of *structuring* discourse that one finds in the psychotic is, Lacan observes, "inaccessible, inert, and stagnant with respect to any dialectic" (*Book III*, 22). What we see clearly in the psychotic is also present, though not in such a dramatic form, in all subjects.

Much of Žižek's argument in *Looking Awry: An Introduction to Jacques Lacan through Popular Culture* explains how all subjects are structured by an isolating *psychotic kernel of enjoyment*. This means that the mechanism that most effectively structures subjects in relation to discourse is itself not in discourse. In *Tarrying With the Negative*, Žižek points out that all subjects in discussion and argument frequently fall back on strangely incommunicable core beliefs or experiences that sustain them in the web of some truth system. These core beliefs may be used in argumentation, but they characteristically prove themselves strangely immune to any dialectic of argumentation. "As we start losing ground in an argument," Žižek observes, "our last recourse is usually to insist that 'despite what has been said, things are essentially what we think them to be'" (134). All our thinking is caught, it seems, in certain instinctive assumptions about reality that are not easily undone by creative language.[1]

Lacanian theory, unlike poststructuralist theory, posits linguistic meaning as operating not simply in the logic of a system of differences that structure the Symbolic but in relation to the effects of what Lacan terms the *Real*. Anika Lemaire explains, "The final signified for which one searches is radically excluded from thought as it concerns an incommensurable dimension, namely the Real" (41). The Real, an "other" place where political identity can find support, is outside discourse. Because it is outside discourse, it can prop up discourse, function as evidentiary support when, in fact, no support is possible. Because of this place outside discourse that supports the attachment to discursive claims, attempts to be persuasive often prove impossible. We simply cannot reach that place where attachments are fixed.

Human social life is a field in which multiple forms of intersubjective relations take place in discourse. Speech fills our life not simply with information but with libidinal relations. We need, demand, or desire things from others, and others do likewise of us. In fully fluid human relations, we do things for others or not, and others do things for us or not. And we accept both relations and limitations in relations. In some cases, however, the demands we make of others, or those others make of us, cannot be compromised. It is as if our very lives were at stake in the fulfillment of a demand. In cases of need, our biological lives are indeed at stake. But in the case of demand, it is not our biological lives that are at stake; it is our symbolic lives. In this context, we must explore how our political lives are intertwined with our symbolic life and our ability to make use of discourse.

As I work on this manuscript, the evening news provides plentiful current examples of lives that are caught up in the discursive life of symbols. In Northern Ireland, the Irish Republican Army refuses the protestants' demand to give up their weapons. In Zimbabwe, white farmers refuse to give up their land to black war veterans. In Miami, Cuban-Americans refuse to give Elian Gonzalez to his father. On the border of Ethiopia and Eritrea, both sides refuse to give up land that they both claim to own. In all but one of these cases, people have died rather than compromise their demands, or more precisely the demands of their leaders. In many of these cases, the people who sacrifice their lives for the demand of their leader gain little for themselves if the demands of their leader are met. Real objects may be gained by nation-states or political groups, but the gain of these real objects is a purely symbolic gain for most of the real people willing to sacrifice their lives for them. Often, as in the case of the Vietnam War, people may come to feel that they have sacrificed too much of themselves for empty symbols, but in the symbolic life of culture, symbols are rarely empty. They are full of the life experience of the subjects whose emotional lives they organize.

In everyday social life, symbols organize the emotional lives of people. Symbols make demands on our time and energy. And yet, for many of us, social demands and their symbolic insistence are susceptible to alteration through a dialectic of social discourse. People are persuaded to rethink what they want and at times give up some of what they want. In the June

2000 meeting between Bill Clinton and Vladimir Putin, the *Washington Post* transcript of their sixteen-point statement reveals an interesting history of both sides as they worked to negotiate difficult demands. Putin comments:

> over the last eight years . . . the efforts of the Russian leadership and of the administration of President Clinton allowed us to always find a way out of these crises with honor, not only to establish good relations, but also to solve problems where we had disagreements. (A11)

When Putin talks about finding a way out, he is talking about symbolic consolations or substitutions for symbolic losses. This shift in symbolic satisfaction is crucial for diplomacy but is often very difficult to achieve.

In social life, people generally make adjustments in what they ask for. Nations engage in political conflicts and accept political compromises; parties lose elections and then plan new campaigns; and spouses argue and reach agreements. Some modes of demand, however, cannot be compromised. Slavoj Žižek describes this rigidity as a kind of drive fixation in the Real that cannot enter dialectic mediation. In these cases, the subject gives up biological existence to satisfy a demand for symbolic recognition.

Demand and Bodily Experience

Žižek, in *Looking Awry*, describes certain fixated compulsions as forms of drive-demand "resistant to dialectic." He explains:

> Demand almost always implies a certain dialectical mediation: we demand something, but what we are really aiming at through this demand is something else—sometimes even the very refusal of the demand in its literality. Along with every demand, a question necessarily rises: "I demand this, but what do I really want by it?" Drive, on the contrary, persists in a certain demand, it is a "mechanical" insistence that cannot be caught up in dialectical trickery. I demand something and I persist in it to the end. (21)

Žižek gives three examples of such demands, which are deaf to dialectical possibility. Žižek calls such demand "pure drive without desire," because desire is, Lacan claims, essentially metonymic in nature. It follows a chain of signifiers, never fully satisfied. Desire, then, initiates dialectic. When desire is frozen, however, dialectic is impossible. Žižek's first example, from Book VII of *The Seminar of Jacques Lacan*, is Antigone's "insistence on a certain unconditional demand on which she is not prepared to give way" (22). The second is Hamlet's father, "who returns from the grave with the demand that Hamlet revenge his infamous death" (22). The third is Arnold Schwarzeneggar in *The Terminator*:

Schwarzenegger plays a cyborg who returns to contemporary Los
Angeles from the future, with the intention of killing the mother of a
future leader. The horror of this figure consists precisely in the fact
that it functions as a programmed automaton who, even when all that
remains of him is metallic, legless skeleton, persists in his demand and
pursues his victim with no trace of compromise or hesitation. The terminator is the embodiment of the drive, devoid of desire. (22)

This fixation, devoid of desire, responds to none of the inducements of intersubjective speech. Such forms of drive-demand are deaf to persuasion
because they can find no objects of satisfaction outside their own forms
of repetition. These drive-demands are also unresponsive to dangers that
threaten bodily existence. Drive-demands are forms of repetition caught in
the body; they operate on meanings that can be spoken by language, but
they cannot be modified by the speech requests or demands of others. In
affirming a symbolic identity, they happily sacrifice biological life. Such
pure forms of drive-demand are relatively rare. They can be heroic, as in
the case of Antigone; uncanny, as in the case of Hamlet's father; or in-
humanly destructive, as in the case of the Terminator.

Subjects caught in the seemingly instinctive programmed behavior of
these kinds of attachments, termed *the dead* by Žižek, are insensitive to
meanings circulating in intersubjective speech. Speech, with its various
inducements to desire, may address this subject, but it will not interpellate
it or change it.

When poststructuralist theory imagines a subject structured by discourse, it has great difficulty making sense of subjects caught in patterns
of repetition unresponsive to dialectic. To understand discourse fully, we
must understand the limitations of discourse. We must understand its inability to move the Terminator, its inability to persuade the anorexic to eat,
and its inability to intervene in those mechanisms of subjectivity that drive
actions inaccessible to dialectic.

Part of this essentially psychoanalytic project would expand Homi
Bhabha's analysis of the nondialectical nature of cultural stereotypes, in
"Interrogating Identity," to see fixated and fetishized thinking as instances
of drive-fixated demands. Just as the fetish is an expression of a sex drive,
fetishist thinking is an expression of bodily experience and thus, in a sense,
not thought at all. Drive-fixated demands, because they are expressions of
the body, seem instinctive and are commonly inaccessible to dialectical
thought. Fetishist thinking, like Helms's claim for a patriotic American
identity, resists any symbolic logic or evidence that would undo an attachment to its own beliefs.

Jesse Helms's opposition to Bill Clinton, for example, can be understood in terms of drive-demands operating in the Lacanian Real. In many ways, the Clinton presidency has been a kind of test case for Rorty's hope to extend logical space through creative language. A liberal baby boomer who opposed the Vietnam War, Bill Clinton was elected president and became the leader of the United States and commander-in-chief of the armed forces. For most Americans, Clinton's position in the symbolic order should have facilitated an extension of logical space, a reforming of political emotions, attitudes, and identities. Bill Clinton should have been the spokesperson for a new and renewed America and the new emotions linked to such hopes. While this may have happened to some extent, it has been more striking to see the extent to which this did not happen. Jesse Helms, for example, is alleged to have advised Clinton that if he came to South Carolina he should bring bodyguards.

This problematic allusion to the possibility of presidential assassination raises serious questions in regard to the linguistic ground of political identity. If Helms is the American patriot that he claims to be, how can he suggest threats to the president of the United States without ceasing to be an American? In a world of symbolic logic and the master signifiers that situate terms such as *patriotic* and *American,* it is clear that a someone who threatens the president is not a good American. Yet it seems clear that Jesse Helms can listen to this purely linguistic analysis and its appeal to honored, established, master signifiers and still maintain himself in the logical contradictions of his alleged political identity. Rorty's dream of logical space needs to be reconsidered in relation to Lacan's claims about the space of the Real. Helms resides not in logical space but in the Lacanian Real when he imagines himself both a good American and a man who wishes to effect the end of an elected president. If Helms is angered by Clinton's anger, his thought is really in the immediate response of his body and he is resistant to a logic that appeals to accepted master signifiers. He is thus isolated from any truth about Clinton's identity that we might attempt to establish through dialectic.

What supports Helms's belief structure? It would be impossible to get to the bottom of this issue, but one persuasive lead would be to trace out his repeated and vehement attack on Clinton as a draft-dodger. Clinton did not fight in Vietnam, and for this reason he cannot be a good American. There seems an emphatic recognition of a certain signifier of identity that Helms sees in Clinton. Helms's logic seems to require that a good American must feel the need to risk death by fighting in a war. Clinton did not show such a drive-demand. Thus, whatever anyone might say, Clinton is not really an American. The word *American* here is not defined in terms of anything logical in the larger realm of language but by a logic of drive-demands that reveal the real truth of someone's identity.

Drive-Demand and the Symbolic

The most durable features of the visibility of the other may be found not in the meanings that circulate in speech but in the meanings whose full significance is read in bodily expression.[2] Drive-demand recognitions offer a particularly convincing experience of evidence for identity because they seem to discover some deeper truth of identity than that found in the symbolic or in the duplicitous representations of speech. Drive-demand shows that whatever others may say about their identities, their real bodily actions reveal their true natures. Bill Clinton may say he is an American, but Jesse Helms is not be deceived by such verbal performances; his knowing is deeper and more insightful. Bill Clinton may claim to be a patriotic American, but Jesse Helms remembers him as a draft-dodger.

Understanding drive-demand encourages us to give attention not to the verbal performances of a person but to bodily performances, especially to the acts of recognition that accompany bodily performances. We know others through the fetish of the stereotype precisely when drive-demand behavior enrages them, makes them laugh, or gives them some telling moment of insight that reduces all their complexity to our bodily response to our experience of their otherness. Our own scopic drive returns again to the pleasure of our insight into the small details of this defining observation. We repeat these moments of deep recognition to others, laughing and forming communities precisely as bodily experience effects of those who can laugh with us and those who, in their bodily pain, are excluded from our laughter and led to bodily anger.

When I was growing up in south Texas, my friends and I would sometimes watch old movies on television that showed East Coast men talking about having a "marvelous time" on vacation. Something about the tone and enthusiasm of those words would crack us up, and we would sarcastically mimic this outlandish behavior as if it were some enormous form of stupidity that we southern boys proudly disdained. Now that I live on the East Coast, I meet regularly with prosperous East Coast intellectuals who go on vacations and come back talking about having had a "marvelous time." Still, after forty years, I cringe when I hear those words and see that form of expression. Though I know that all these performance games are purely arbitrary, I still feel acts of allegiance in my body to the blue-collar, working-class background of my youth.

Jokes, in this sense, become prime sites at which language structures interact with drive-demand structures. When we hear a joke, we do not pause to make a decision about whether we want to laugh or not. We simply respond to the "meaning" of the joke. But jokes have meanings that are not quite the same as the meanings of everyday discourse. Jokes demand bodily response from us, and thus "mean" in terms of an involuntary bodily response (some might be prompted to call these responses *instinctual*) that bears witness to how we have been structured by bodily drive-demands. Jokes work only when we get their meanings not as conceptual responses (pure signifiers) but as bodily responses, meanings outside discourse that cannot be said but can only be performed by drive-demand structures in the body. Jokes that are funny to some groups make other groups anxious. Jokes, like symptoms, manage anxiety, and the people we laugh with are the people we identify with. The opposite is also true. People who do not feel anxiety when we feel anxiety are people we cannot trust. They are comfortable with material that threatens us. They are thus allied with our enemies, they are "others"—all those imaginary enemies that populate our inner world. We read these signs of what is *us* and who is *other* in daily messages that reveal anxiety and laughter. These messages reveal primary structures of drive-demand identity that are deeper than the meanings we entertain in language.

A particular joke, a pure fixed linguistic message, will produce different bodily responses depending on the bodily subjectivity of the hearer. We can feel the pleasure of laughing with others, we can feel the pain and shame of being laughed at, or we may not get the joke and feel general embarrassment. The popularity of ethnic jokes reveals how ethnic communities use humor to constitute individuals at the level of drive-demand. We slowly join a group as we learn involuntary bodily responses that define us in opposition to other groups. From early in our life, groups make demands of us to laugh with them, eat their food, appreciate their models of beauty, and feel repulsion toward things they despise. When our performances earn their approval, they smile at us with recognition. We show the first step in any kind of understanding; we understand what the Other wants.

In Lacanian terms, we are all trained by the demands the Other makes of us. Robert Samuels describes the Lacanian anal stage as one in which the subject is asked to comply with the demand of the Other. The response to demand produces a wholesale organization in subjective experience. Demand means that the subject must "control and organize its world and perceptions through the mastering of its body and the manipulation of the object of desire" (49). In order to be toilet trained, children must learn to control their bodies. The demand for bodily control is not an argument that is won by good arguments; it is won by the force of the parent's demand:

"If you want my love, you will comply." The response to demand reshapes and informs the very experience of the body. Internal experience that operated according to involuntary processes now become disciplined. Experiences of discomfort that impede toilet training are simply repressed. Mastery of the body gives pride; failure of mastery give shame.

Other forms of compliance to demand can be understood in terms of similar forms of bodily mastery. In the Milgram experiment, for example, experiences of anxiety in the face of the hurt victim become, for many subjects, lost to experience when they comply with demand. Demand responds to the discomfort of ambivalence by making one pole of the experience simply absent to experience.

Jokes train the body by force of demand, just as toilet training does. We laugh with those we want to identify with. If we do not share laughter, we may feel the bodily shame of being laughed at by them. We thus define our self-image by learning to be the one who laughs at another. We show in this manner that we have learned the unconscious demands made of us: we control our world, master our bodies, and properly manipulate the objects of our desires.

To be a member of a group, it is important to master a variety of involuntary bodily experiences. It is important to be subjected to the demands of a master who transmits the rules of culture. These rules cannot be violated without offending the group with which we claim identity. Any group membership, thus, may require certain preferences, styles in terms of which we look at, and are looked at, by others. Often, these drive-demand preferences work in conjunction with written laws that define group behavior. Thus it may be unlawful for Muslims to eat pork or Christians to be homosexual, or unlawful for a woman to wear pants in a particular institution. As we all know, these laws by themselves do not *create* drive-demand preferences, since cultures, which teach these laws, also produce people who, to various degrees, may feel driven to break them. Learning the law of drive-demand is not equivalent to learning the meaning of signification. Drive-demand is learned unconsciously in our identifications, in our responses to the demand of the Other.

I argue that the visibility of the other, our most immediate sense response to human otherness, is formed in terms of drive repetitions. Others are *others* not because they are *represented* as such by symbolic signifiers but because of the way in which drive, as an experience of the body, reacts to signifiers of bodily difference.

Because drive-demand operates in the Real of the body, it is fixed and unresponsive to the dialectic of the symbolic. This fixed nature of drive can be explained in two ways. The first part of the explanation expands Homi

Bhabha's point that "one has to see the surveillance of colonial power as functioning in relation to the regime of the scopic drive . . . the drive that represents the pleasure of seeing" (76). The scopic drive sets in place a generally unconscious and persistent pattern of *looking for* some signifier of bodily signification. The scopic drive sets in place, in advance of either thought or language, a repetition in the body of the observer, a certain anticipated pleasure of looking for something.

The second part of this explanation describes how other drives set in place a pattern of finding *what* one looks for. Here, drive repeatedly discovers something in the drive body of the other. This particular difference in drive between oneself and the other functions as the whole meaning of the other. In this manner, infinitely varied and small differences become reduced in complexity, and a particular person's nature acquires meaning only in terms of an inflated and fetishly fixated signification that is a sign of drive difference. The other, thus, has food preferences, or sexual preferences or play preferences that in their concrete form are not simply *different* in some world of abstract thought but definitive and *dramatic* in a world of lived bodily sensations. The other embodies in bodily drive sensations what observers must reject from their own subjectivity. Those sensations threaten the observer's own psychotic kernel of enjoyment.

Bhabha argues that "the stereotype impedes the circulation and articulation of the signifier of 'race' as anything other than its fixity as racism. We always already know that blacks are licentious, Asiatics duplicitous" (75). The discovery of the other always takes pleasure in the recognition of some characteristic otherness of the drive body. The other always talks funny, eats funny food, has an odd style of sexual display, laughs at jokes that do not make good sense. In others' acting out ethnic drives that define their identities, they become the object of our jokes. They are caught helpless, represented by their own drive repetition, which shames them in our eyes, even as we, caught in our own drive, laugh at our perceptions of them. The Other is the one who, like an Italian, puts on too much cologne to attract women; who, like a Mexican, hankers for *menudo* (a hot chile soup made from animal intestines), even when we (non-Hispanics) find it disgusting; who, like a Scotsman, hangs on to every penny even when his wealth could replace his shoddy clothes with new and respectable ones.

The Other of the Symbolic

The point of this analysis is to insist that while poststructuralist theory has made important contributions to our understanding of language, it has also oversimplified our understanding of signification. Jacques-Alain Miller argues that differences that matter in the recognition of the other reflect differences in *jouissance* not differences in signification per se. The violent hatreds generated by racism, for example, are grounded, not in any logic of the signifier, per se, but in the conflicts of disavowed forms of *jouissance* that are in bodily experience not mental representations.

At the level of the symbolic, of sheer representation, there can be a perception of abstract difference as in the difference between the number six and the number seven, but this difference is not enough to ground a powerful emotional feeling. In signification itself, then, there can be no real ground for antagonism toward the other. Miller argues:

> no one can ground the alterity of the Other in the signifier, since the very law of the signifier implies that one can always be substituted for the other and vice versa. . . . In this dimension, there is a kind of democracy, an equality, a community, a principle of peace. (79)

Unlike semantic difference, which can be programmed into computers and implies contrast but not struggle, the difference of racism is a real antagonism felt in bodily sensation. It is not an abstraction, like a math problem coded in a pure symbolic logic. It is a powerful emotional experience. Its logic operates not according to the logic of the symbolic, as Lacan defined the term, but according to the real and the drives, in what Lacanians term the *jouissance* of the body.

While poststructuralist theory imagines intersubjective speech as a logic of the symbolic able to alter drive structure easily, Lacanian theory emphasizes the difficulty of such an ambition. The logic of the symbolic will have little effect on drive-demand because such experience is written in the body. It operates from a system outside the direct effects of symbolic argument. It is that point of attachment we can see in arguments when people, attached to feelings, sensations, or seeming empty and unfathomable patterns of repetition, will not give way to new thoughts or sensations as a result of what seems to be overwhelming evidence for the need for such shift.

Drive-demands are the effect of representations, but they are not representations in the same manner as language is representation. Drive-demands operate from the Real of the body, and they are not easily influenced by language representations that operate in the symbolic and the imaginary. The Lacanian systems of the Real, Imaginary, and Symbolic exist at different levels and operate according to different internal logics. One can imagine this metaphor of structural levels with respect to the computer. Just as one cannot, while within a word-processing program, type the words *eject the disk* and expect a disk to be ejected by the computer, one cannot reach the drives that animate the Terminator by saying, "It is time

to relax and see a movie." This logic or fantasy will not be introduced to
the drive-demand, and it will not operate the Terminator because the language that operates the Terminator has been sedimented in the Real, at another level within the machinery of subjectivity.

Mourning and the Path to Dialectic

Cultures become violent whenever two groups with opposing drive-demands resort to violence as a solution to an impasse in demand. Cultures
become stagnant whenever established practices of demand become accepted without question. Cultural progress proceeds whenever oppressive
demands pass into negotiations that displace their effect. Because demand
plays a significant role in shaping human communities, writing classes
should seek to understand and respond to expressions of demand.

I have suggested in the course of this book that a particularly difficult
problem in making writing classes responsive to political issues is the problem of fixated identity positions. I suggested in chapter 3 that some identity
positions held in place by demand can sometimes be changed by new demands. Such changes, I argued, have doubtful value. First, they characteristically generate considerable resistance in students allied with conflicting
demands. This turns the classroom into a site at which two clearly defined
political positions battle for mastery. Dialectic may be generated, and some
students may choose new masters, but such a process does not generate a
dialectic that loosens identity fixations. Second, while some students may
adopt better political positions, this change, in the long run, does not help
the students who accept these demands. This is true because this kind of
training does not improve a subject's ability to interact with the desires of
others. It merely trains a student to accept the claims of authority figures.
Social justice, I insist, is not a matter of simply teaching a correct ideology;
it is a matter of responding justly to human suffering, to expressions of desire and need. It requires an attunement in the social field of discourse that
minimizes the defensive distortions social beings use in responding to the
needs and desires of others.

In the first part of this chapter, I argued that those attachments held in
place by drive-fixated bodily experience will not be responsive to verbal
dialectic at all. Clashes with these demands will only produce mutual aggression. There are, however, still other forms of attachments, heavily invested with emotion, that can, with work, respond to dialectical mediation. I describe this work as the work of mourning, and it is here, I think,
that the work of composition can be helped by a psychoanalytic grasp of
human subjectivity.

The work of composition required to undo grief attachments does not involve the usual academic discipline of memorization, skill-solving, or the transfer of knowledge. It is, instead, an emotional task of considerable complexity.

Theories of rhetoric and argument often acknowledge the importance of emotion in the writer's life. Good texts, for example, often observe that emotions present unique difficulties and opportunities for persuasion and reason. Lunsford's and Ruszkiewicz's *everything's an argument* points out that, "Emotional appeals are powerful tools for influencing what people think and believe" (43). Lunsford and Ruszkiewicz suggest that emotions can "build bridges" between a speaker and the audience, and they suggest that humor can sometimes be used to put skittish readers at ease. Much good advice is offered to writers in *everything's an argument,* but like most texts, it sees emotion in terms of the immediate context of a rhetorical exercise and fails to recognize the depth, complexity, and temporal insistence of the emotional life of the reader and writer.

Classic perspectives on rhetoric undervalue emotion because it lacks reason. Postmodernists undervalue emotion because it seems merely an effect of discourse and social practice. It is now time, as Lynn Worsham argues eloquently in "Going Postal: Pedagogic Violence and the Schooling of Emotion," to take emotion seriously: "our most urgent political and pedagogical task" she says, is "the fundamental reeducation of emotion" (216). In suggesting that we must seek to develop an anti-ideological ethic, I do not suggest that we seek an escape from emotion but that we seek to cultivate an emotional life in direct emotional dialogue with all other people not just the people we identify with. My appeal for a free circulation of desire involves a commitment to equal opportunities for the expression and communication of emotion. More specifically, we must find ways to experience and respond in an ethically responsible manner to the emotions of those who, as an effect of ideological practice, have been excluded from this dialogue.

When we see education in relation to emotion, we must see the concept of desire in more expansive terms. Lynn Worsham observed in 1991 that, "For some time now a major strand of thought in literary and cultural studies has been focused on detailing forms of pleasure and desire."[3] French theorists such a Lacan, Kristeva, and more recently Slavoj Žižek and Judith Butler, have been widely influential in emphasizing the formative effects of *jouissance* on culture and subjectivity. Composition theorists from bell hooks to Victor Vitanza have supported a pedagogy that endorses the free movement of desire in thought. There has even been support for the erotic element in pedagogy from Jane Gallop and others. Thus far, I have framed my own argument in terms of a circulation of desire necessary for social justice and democratic politics, and I have drawn on some of the rhetoric of these writers.

Let me now place this emphasis on desire in a larger, more important, and, I think, more concrete context. Both Lacan and Freud suggest that we cannot adequately imagine desire if we do not understand its relation to loss and anxiety. Desire is a response to loss and a response to anxiety. We seek to replace those objects (both people and things) that we have lost, and we seek to find remedies for those things that make us anxious. When desire is relatively free, we have relative liberty of thought in seeking useful solutions to real problems. Fixations of desire are often effects of anxieties that cannot be managed. When desires are fixated, we seek remedies for imaginary problems and find imaginary solutions for real problems.

To free desire does not mean so much to experience new desires or to desire more intensely as it means to allow desire to work as a metaphoric and metonymic structure necessary for the intersubjective possibilities of meanings. If teachers want to help students generate and respond to desire, they must take responsibility not simply for desire but also for loss and anxiety, that ground where desire first becomes mobilized, directed, and invested.

My emphasis on the importance of desire for discourse, then, is not a simple call for the liberation of desire. Because people form libidinal investments in linguistic constructions, optimum flexibility in discourse use requires painful acts of libidinal disinvestment that analysts describe as mourning. Democratic societies are not formed by the simple pursuit of pleasure, but they may be fostered by more egalitarian practices in the recognition, circulation, and elaboration of desire. These forms of intersubjective interaction require the development of less fixated forms of attachment and less defensive habits of thought.

When we imagine an education process that works on emotion, we must imagine a very slow process. Often teachers experience their greatest successes when they see students slowly begin to open up to new and more complex ideas in the final papers they write in a course. This advance in critical thinking is also an advance in feeling, and it is one that follows a process of mourning. To understand the emotional work of writing then, we must understand the emotional work of mourning.

Giving Up Strong Beliefs Is a Form of Mourning

Jeffrey Berman's *Diaries to an English Professor* depicts examples of students who come to change deeply held beliefs and feelings as a result of the gradual effects of writing, reading, and reflection. I will show how mourning is important to this process and I want to call attention to the distinctive nature of mourning that can help teachers help their students make progress in mourning. Written to show how students can change profoundly as a result of journal writing, Berman's book shows how difficult emotional change is. In one chapter, a student writes in his journal about a letter he has recently written to his father. The student, Paul, quotes from his letter and thereby reveals in his journal that he has changed his understanding of the relationship he wants with his divorced father. He writes:

> My point is, Dad, that I have finally aborted the idea that not having
> relations with a living father is acceptable. This view might have protected me through my adolescent years, but I can no longer be shielded
> by something I no longer believe. I think the time has come for us to
> meet again—or at least for us to now talk. (76)

Paul's change in feeling merits attention. It is an example of the kind of beneficial influence writing teachers sometimes have on students. Charles Bazerman expresses the feelings of many writing instructors when he observes, "There seems to be no other form of teaching at the university that grants the teacher such personal knowledge of a student as a sufferer and maker of his or her own life" (67). In Berman's student, we see him reveal himself as both someone who suffers and someone who, in the midst of his suffering, acts to remake his own life. This is always, and necessarily, a dramatic moment for teachers. We see in the student's diary an important change in a passionately held belief, brought about, the student says, by his English course.

What we see expressed in an instant of thought is an effect of many months of conflicted and painful reflection. In his letter to his father, the student gives credit for his change in belief to a "five-month study of the family as a social organization." But in his diary entry, the student gives credit for his change to his English course. The wording he uses to express his change in belief is significant. He says that he has decided to "abort an idea." His former idea, as he expresses it, is a child. In changing his beliefs, the student "kills" a child. What is curious about this wording is that something that most of us would see in terms of a net gain, the gain of a relationship to a biological father, the student sees and experiences in terms of a loss. In terms of the metaphor, he loses a child as he regains a relationship with his father. It is to this experience of loss as the ground of personal change that I now want to give particular attention.

All changes in deeply held beliefs involve an experience of loss or mourning. If writing teachers are to help in this activity of changing deeply invested feelings, they would do well to understand the mourning process. Too often, we consider thought as a process that can effortlessly move the elements of signification in all possible logical permutations. Changes in meaning, however, are not the effect of instant change in signification. Important changes in meaning require significant changes in feeling. These changes are not instant permutations in relationships of signifiers; they require slow changes in libidinal investments. This change is not slow because the words that represent this change cannot be formed instantly, but because the necessary changes in feeling (necessary for the words to be personally meaningful) are painful, and the acts necessary to overcome this pain require it to be taken up slowly.

When people come to change important feelings, something must be given up, and this is a painful experience. In "Mourning and Melancholia," Freud argues that the pain of mourning is not equivalent to the pain of lacking something. Rather, the pain of mourning is a peculiar pain occasioned by a giving up of something we have *had* either in truth or in fantasy. *Having* something is always a curious imaginary relationship. Yet the work of mourning shows that all imaginary states of mind are not equal. Some imaginary representations are owned and some are not. Owned representations have durability because they have been invested with libido or emotion.

The *work* of mourning, Freud says, consists of *withdrawing* libido from its attachment to an object. Such work, Freud points out, is hard and painful work because the self "never willingly abandons a libido position, even when a substitute is already beckoning" (126). Freud's point here is worth emphasis: what is painful is not the *fact* of not having something but the *effort* required to withdraw libido from something that you have *already* (in some imaginary sense) had.

According to psychoanalytic theory, the work of mourning performs some particular function that is beneficial to the mourner. Therapy provides people with skills that, as they advance the labor of mourning, improve mental health and their ability to respond flexibly and responsibly to the demands and desires of others.

Part of the difficulty of mourning is that its work progresses in proportion to a mourner's willingness to suffer the experience of grief. Grief is not a thought; it is a painful bodily feeling. Just as drive-demands make a claim on the body, so mourning makes a claim on the body. Erich Lindemann in "Symptomatology and Management of Grief," a now classic paper, observes:

> The picture shown by persons in acute grief is remarkably uniform.
> Common to all is the following syndrome: sensation of somatic distress
> occurring in waves lasting from twenty minutes to an hour at a time, a

feeling of tightness in the throat, choking with shortness of breath, need for sighing, and an empty feeling in the abdomen, lack of muscular power, and an intense subjective distress described as tension or mental pain. The patient soon learns that these waves of discomfort can be precipitated by visits, by mentioning the deceased, and by receiving sympathy. (19)

Sometimes grief initiates bodily changes that pose real medical risks. Lindemann lists a group of psychosomatic conditions, predominantly ulcerative colitis, rheumatoid arthritis, and asthma, that are often triggered by loss. One study showed "thirty three out of forty-one patients with ulcerative colitis developed their disease in close time relationships to the loss of an important person" (25).

The Bodily Pain of Changing Representations

The enormous and painful work of mourning helps us change our internal representations of the world. Confronted with the death of a person close to us, we must recognize that the person is no longer present. This fact is, in theory, something we can accomplish in an instant. We might say, "Dad is dead," and yet this simple fact is not at all simple for human experience. The considerable study of mourning, much of it done after the devastating experiences of World War II, shows that humans resist the truth of human loss. Dead people do not die easily in our imaginations; they continue to live in our internal representations.

A person mourned or even an identity mourned is not, as in processes of logical thought, imagined as a whole and discrete entity. Mourning, instead, repeatedly and insistently fails to honor the boundaries between people and those things in both the inner world of the self and the real outer world that remind us of them. A person mourned, for example, is not an entity but a blurred field of figurations, a composition knitted together by a collage of images, feelings, and associated ideas, all present but dispersed through various layers of the mind. To be mourned, this composition of figurations must be abandoned memory-piece by memory-piece. According to Freud, each of these elements is cathected by libido, and the *work* of mourning, "painful" and "absorbing" work, Freud says, consists in bringing all these various and sundry elements, memories, images, hopes, into consciousness to sever the attachment of libido (241).

Freud argues the work of mourning proceeds as "each single one of the memories and expectations [of the deceased] in which libido is bound . . . is brought up and hypercathected" (239). This seems surprising but also empirically true. A former student once told me that in his village in China, funeral painters go to the family of the deceased to compose a final picture.

The painter asks what the deceased looked like. The family, upon this request, turns about in their memory an image. Their task, part of the ceremony of mourning, is to picture each aspect of the dead person. What was the head like? The eyes, the nose, the mouth, the ears? When the task of remembering is complete, the picture can be painted. Freud's description of the piecemeal activity of mourning helps explain what happens at funerals. Members of the family of the deceased enter the church to pay last respects to the deceased. At various moments during the funeral ceremony, they achieve a measure of composure. Typically, however, the ongoing process of the funeral ceremony breaks this composure down. Thoughts evoked by a eulogy release new and fresh memories of the deceased. These newly discovered memories trigger new dimensions of pain, and those in acute mourning weep. When the eulogy is over, composure may be regained, but as members of the family approach the coffin, new reservoirs of grief flood forward. The face of the deceased, seen now from yet another perspective charged with memory, triggers a new outbreak of tears. It is as if each distinct image and memory released new sources of grief and attachment that have not yet been emptied. Freud's observations seem correct. Each memory image of the deceased is invested with libido that cannot be withdrawn without painful and absorbing work of memory and recollection. People cannot be mourned until the totality of their representational calculus is traced, recovered, and given up through the painful process of mourning's figurations.

Freud describes mourners as those who "abrogates" interest in the outside world as they attend to the painful demands of an internal world. Much of the power and mystery of mourning pertains to the fact that while this process instinctively *expresses* unrealistic assumptions, the essential *work* of mourning requires a curious sort of labor, both intellectual and emotional, that teaches us to *overcome* unrealistic assumptions. Mourning is an especially interesting process because it seems to empower a faculty that links the figures of the imagination to certain conceptions of reality. Mourning labors to bind us to reality. It does so by policing the imagination of the grieving mind, mercilessly stamping on its various images the truth of a painful fact: what we desire is not.

It is clear that people mourn, but it is not clear how exactly people are attached to people. Attachment is in the mind and, according to Freud, in the libido. But where does the glue of libido adhere? Where are the roots by which libido extends into the essence of other things?

If we assume that libido is somehow attached to people, we must ask, What are people? How are they, in our attachments to them, present to us? How are they *figured* or *represented* by the conscious and unconscious mind as belonging to us? Discussing the mourning process, Freud himself makes some rather surprising observations. He suggests, for example, that people are not known, held, or lost by the self in whole, complete, and discrete forms. Instead, people are composed piecemeal of memory images, ideas, feelings, and even associations.

Donald Murray, an esteemed writing instructor and professor emeritus at the University of New Hampshire, describes a moment when mourning the death of his daughter is a conversation with a bird: "Lee, I am sure, was with me the other morning when I whistled at a bird and it whistled back. For a quarter of a mile the bird and I continued our conversation" (145). Murray writes as if he thought the bird were his daughter. Such thinking would, in normal conditions be considered psychotic, but in mourning, such thinking is common. The relationship between birds and daughters is purely a relationship of association. Yet it seems that it is precisely at the level of association—and imagination—that mourning can have profound effects.

As a process, mourning has a strong kinship with that mental activity Freud termed the *primary processes,* mental activity that is heavily funded by the imagination and does not acknowledge the reality of the outside world. Mourning is a process tied so strongly to powerful internal images that it does not recognize the real boundaries of people. It spills over into powerful feelings attached to associated objects, places, sounds, smells, and concepts. Mourning, thus, is a process absolutely and inextricably involved with imagination and figuration.

Yet our appreciation of mourning's involvement with figuration only obscures our understanding of the most decisive effects of the mourning process. Mourning responds to figurations, but in *responding* to figurations, it works to *construct* the real world as we represent it to ourselves and are attached to it in our minds.

It is a curious fact that mourning exists, in part, because people do not want to accept changes in their internal worlds. They do not want to live in the real world. Mourning is a situation in which, because of the pain of loss, people are especially tempted to rely on their imaginations and deny their perceptions of the real.

In order to effect changes in these internal representations, we must suffer bodily pain for a considerable length of time. Erich Lindemann argues:

> The duration of a grief reaction seems to depend upon the success
> with which a person does the *grief work,* namely emancipation from
> the bondage to the deceased, readjustment to the environment in which
> the deceased is missing, and the formation of new relationships. One of

the big obstacles to this work seems to be the fact that many patients try
to avoid the intense distress connected with the grief experience and to
avoid the expression of emotion necessary for it. (21)

All of us, faced with profound loss, are tempted to deny loss and insist that
what we love still survives. As everyone now seems to know, the first normal human response to loss is denial. If we are told about an unexpected
loss, we deny the truth of the claim. Freud points out that the ego is always
tempted to ignore the painful messages of reality and hallucinate pleasures
that are not available. Bowlby describes the mourner as one "repeatedly
seized, whether he knows it or not, by an urge to call for, to search for and
to recover the lost person" (27–28). Many accounts of mourning describe
the grieving mind as one constantly expecting to see the deceased person
reappear. Hallucination is not uncommon. Over time, however, if the work
of mourning proceeds properly, the mourner gives up seeking the impossible and comes to recognize that death is permanent and inalterable.

An understanding of mourning is important for rhetoric because it presents a quintessential case in which changes in the world require changes
in the self. It presents a situation in which accepting changes in the world
requires a usually difficult change in the self and in those internal representations that make the self comfortable in the world.

Many therapists point out that the proper object of mourning is both
outside the self, and, paradoxically, inside the self. The center of mourning
is a "void" somewhere or somehow in us. Mourning requires not simply
recognition that an other person is gone but recognition that there is a
persistently painful wound or emptiness located within the self. George
Pollock calls attention to an "inner" pain that a grieving patient seeks to
avoid: "She gradually recognized that to mourn was to acknowledge the
nothingness of her mother, and this meant emptiness inside her" (349).
This emphasis on an inner emptiness, an emptiness within the self introduced by the work of mourning, should prompt us to reconsider some of
our assumptions about mourning. Mourning has no clear center because
it is itself but one aspect of a larger figurative system of presence that supports both the sense of self and the sense of things. Mourning betrays the
workings of some mechanism within both the self and language that, operating on language and memory, endows and withdraws the rhetoric of
presence.

This is true, Lacanian theory insists, because the self is, from the first,
essentially an anxious emptiness. It is a vortex that relieves the pain of
emptiness as it forms attachments through a collection of internalized objects. The self is not a direct experience of the body; it is the final effect of

the series of mental images and experiences that work to represent it. This self then is of the same stuff as those images of others in which we live comfortably at home and in relation to people and things that make us feel centered and comfortable.

The work done by analysts suggest that a mourner's experience of emptiness not only *informs* painful memories of lost people but also, paradoxically, *cultivates* a subtle representational grid that defines diverse and complicated aspects of self experience. Mourning, in short, shows itself as part of a system of meaning, or a system of rhetoric, that not only informs the *emptiness* of the things we imagine to be lost but also supports the *substantiveness* of the things we imagine to be present.

In *Book II* of *The Seminar,* Lacan argues that the world the self lives in, as opposed to a world inhabited by other subjects, is a world constructed by desire: "Desire is a relation of being to lack. This lack is the lack of being properly speaking. It isn't the lack of this or that, but lack of being whereby the being exists" (223). Sounding much like Heidegger, Lacan emphasizes that we have *being* in so far as desire constructs for us an internal self-image and world of internal representations. "Being comes into existence as an exact function of this lack," he says. "Being attains a sense of self in relation to being as a function of this lack, in the experience of desire" (224).

If social-constructionist theory argues that the self and the world are constructions, Lacan would readily agree. But this does not mean that every use of language leads to a social construction. In order for personal representations to operate as meaning, they must be invested with desire. To disinvest social constructions, one must do more than use language or be rational, one must do the work of withdrawing desire from representations. This work is the work of mourning.

Psychoanalytic interpretation is a complex thing, but in a very literal way, it might be considered a strategy for pursuing tasks of mourning that a patient instinctively resists. Patients, for example, come to an analyst because they have problems: there are things they cannot do or think as easily as they would like. Because these things cannot be easily thought or entertained, they prevent the patient from responding to reality with full flexibility and complexity. The analyst aids patients by helping them to understand recurrent problems that they themselves cannot grasp. The analyst, we say, interprets patients to themselves. We normally equate interpretation with something like explanation, but we realize how inadequate this definition is when we consider the difficulties of how explanations work in psychoanalysis. In many cases, an analyst very quickly sees and understands problems that are only too obvious. Analysts, after a longer time, may come to feel very confident of their understanding of a patient's problem. But analysts know that they cannot simply *explain* this problem to the patient. Interpretations do not work in terms of the usual communicative functions of language. Interpretations need proper timing, emphasis, and preparation. A patient can understand an explanation only through a complicated process of suffering and reflecting. The verbal structures that *can* accomplish the work of interpretation do not achieve this goal in and of themselves. The verbal structures of explanation, when they work, must be properly timed and orchestrated; they are not so much *presented* to the patient as *performed* for the patient. To understand the obvious but hidden message of these verbal structures, patients must make certain investments in their representational possibilities. What seems necessary for understanding, it seems, is the binding and unbinding of libido. What is necessary, in short, is a certain task of mourning responding to a verbal structure.

Unlike explanations about how to assemble bicycles, explanations of people's history of desire cannot be delivered in clear, simple, and unambiguous language. There is a marked resistance within patients to the ideas they are presented. Patients resist the new ideas because they hold on to certain other ideas that are more meaningful. But when we say that these ideas are more meaningful, we do not say that they offer a better *explanation* of the patient's experience. These ideas, as patients come to feel later, are, in fact, a *bad* explanation of events. But these ideas seem good and *meaningful,* because, through a curious logic of mental life, patients cannot abandoned them—cannot mourn their loss. To abandon such ideas would mean to introduce too much emptiness into the self.

What happens in a dramatic way to people in mourning also happens in a less dramatic way to people who are faced with information that requires changes in the their understanding of the world. They, too, like people in mourning, find that abandoning comfortable ideas introduces too much emptiness into the self.

From Theory to Practice

To imagine how classrooms can provide resources for the work of negotiation and mourning, we might begin by examining work already done in this area. Jeffrey Berman's *Diaries to an English Professor* records the writing done by students in the 1980s and 1990s. Berman asked his students to make diary responses as a way of investigating the ideas that developed in a course that talked about literature from a psychoanalytic perspective. Berman observed that, "Although writing about personal problems was sometimes painful, the students felt better afterward and were convinced that writing was therapeutic" (3). Berman's course is avowedly Freudian, psychoanalytic, and self-exploratory. The evidence he gives of its usefulness is hard to controvert. He claims that those students who "revealed traumatic events said that writing the unspeakable was a turning point in their lives" (3).

After reading the book, I find that the strongest argument supporting Berman's claim comes from the student writers themselves. It is clear that they wrestled with deeply personal problems and made headway in their ability to respond positively to new ideas. The afterword, written by former graduate student Maryanne Hannan, records an initial discomfort with Berman's practice overcome by gradual appreciation:

> Sure, diary writing can be therapeutic. Sure, diaries shared with an empathic reader have even more potential to be therapeutic. But is a college classroom an acceptable place for this activity? . . . Eventually, albeit reluctantly, I came to conclude that the classroom is not incidental to the process. It is at the very heart of it. (268)

Berman's central argument is that journal writing of the sort he encourages changes students. It works, however, precisely by not asking students to change. Instead, it simply lets students speak honestly, and in the emotionally charged silence in which students listen to each other, they come to define themselves differently. Later in this chapter, I will discuss the important role silence can play in a dialectic. For now, I want to simply suggest that Berman rejects the discourse of the master and the discourse of the university and uses, instead, the discourse of the analyst.

I have said that Berman's course is psychoanalytic, but I should emphasize that Berman, as a matter of principle, does not psychoanalyze his students. Diaries are required, but Berman's only responses are supportive ones. He writes in the margin comments such as "Interesting" or "Important"; he does not make value judgments or transgress the boundaries needed to maintain student/teacher relationships. If students change, it is not a response to the demands of teacher but because of a journal and the student's relation to the journal.

It would be interesting to know what James Berlin would make of Berman's classes. Although he does not think of himself as a political activist, there are a great deal of race, class, and gender problems addressed in the diaries. In the chapter "Sexual Disclosures," Berman introduces statistics about male abuse of women:

> In a recent survey of 114 undergraduates, a large majority agree with the following statements: "I prefer relatively small women" (93.7 percent agreement); "I like to dominate a woman" (91.3 percent); "I enjoy

the conquest part of sex" (86.1 percent); "Some women look like they're just asking to be raped" (83.5 percent). (200)

Berman observes that generally the men in his class do not write on these issues. Part of his policy is that he does not require students to write about anything. They have complete freedom to explore what they want. Nonetheless, Berman finds that, on average, 30% of his students write about sexual experiences or feelings that they find problematic. Many of these entries are about harassment, homosexual identities, or homophobia. One student wrote a disturbing entry about the sexual assault of a female student by fraternity members. Berman writes that he was "horrified" by the diary entry but unsure about how to handle it in the class. He says:

> As a rule I do not read a diary aloud if it might make either the diarist or another student in the class feel defensive. Scott was honest enough to admit that his first response upon hearing his friend's story was laughter—and he was sensitive enough to realize later that his amusement was inappropriate. (201)

Berman argues that he does not judge his students when they make journal entries. Even in writing the book, as he points out, he tries to be careful with judgmental terms. While he earlier described his response to the entry about sexual assault with a feeling of horror, he is very careful in the paragraph after the quote to control his judgment of his student's initial amusement. It is, Berman says, "inappropriate."

Berman did not offer a strong judgment of the student's entry, but another student in the class, a woman, did. She wrote:

> In my diary for this week, I'd like to comment on a diary read last week about a bunch of frat guys who cheered on one of their so-called brothers as he raped a girl. When I heard that diary, I thought I'd be sick. I was so repulsed that this actually happened. It's not as though I don't know that rape is a common occurrence, especially on college campuses, but since I've been in school, I haven't heard of that many. The person who wrote that diary, if I can remember clearly, didn't use the word "rape." Why? In my opinion, that girl was raped in every sense of the word, and what's worse is that a bunch of guys cheered it on! The thought makes me want to throw up! I don't care if the girl went willingly to that guy's dorm or apartment. I don't know of many girls, or guys, for that matter, who haven't gone back willingly to someone's room for whatever the reason. That's no explanation to rape someone. This sadist obviously had the whole escapade planned for the sole reason of humiliating the poor girl. (202)

Berman's examples of controversial journal entries raise most of the issues I have tried to develop so far in this chapter in theoretical terms. We find in the writer of the first entry a clear sense drive-demand. The writer laughs at what his friends find funny. This drive-demand shows an attachment to a primary identity. The student's laughter makes him a member of a particular social group that treats women as objects and not as people. The laughter might be called *instinctive* because it reveals, some would say, how the writer honestly feels about women as opposed to what he might say if he were called on to speak in front of people who expect him to repeat their own values. I suggest that the writer is not purely identified with a drive-demand; there is a slight critical attitude shown to the friends, "It is hard for me to understand why people need to make someone else suffer in the process" (243). The writer's laughter is admitted as if it were a confession, but there is also much ambivalence in the entry, as if the writer were unsure of his own position even as he wrote.

I suspect that most of us not part of fraternity culture find it difficult to imagine how anyone could laugh at being told this story. If we feel angry with this laughter, as most readers will, I suspect our response is also an expression of drive-demand. The behavior described is clearly sadistic. As teachers, however, we need to find a way to bring the writer's drive-demand into dialectic. If we move too quickly to demand the "right" attitude, we may trigger the defenses that make that attitude very difficult to generate.

The kind of reworking of feeling that Berman's journals offer is, I believe, more effective than most political training offered by many politically progressive teachers. The students' entries offer a dialogue between the male writer and the female writer, and they show how people do, and can, move from one identification to another when they are provided both the freedom and the logical space to examine themselves and their relations to others. Let us review how this movement takes place. The writer himself suggests that the shift from laughter to unease involves changes in a series of representations: "My friends aren't rapists. In fact, the word 'rape' didn't come to mind until I thought of all the implications of their actions. This girl was humiliated in front of them, and they loved it." The first point at which the student finds meaning anchored in relation to this act is a reference made to his friends. "My friends aren't rapists," he says.

Why did he say that his friends were not rapists? Freudians might insist that this is a perfect example of denial. The student is really showing in the unconscious that something is true when he claims overtly that it is not true. Let me advance a somewhat different claim as another component of this undoubtedly overdetermined articulation. It is precisely the writer's attachment to these people that makes them, through some irrational but very powerful logic, something other than rapists. The word *rapist* has negative implications. A *friend*, however, is generally a good person. In the thinking of the unconscious, value judgments tend to be in black and white, and they are simple reflections of our attachments in the world. Friends, as long as they are friendly, are good and *therefore* (as the unconscious thinks) not rapists.

It seems to me that if we look at the male's diary entry by itself, it is difficult to determine where this student stands in relation to sexual politics. On the one hand, there is an overt attempt to be on the right side, when the writer says, "it is hard for me to understand why people need to make someone else suffer." And yet the entry never fully charges the friends with rape. The closest the student comes to thinking this is in the passive sentence, "the word 'rape' didn't come to mind until I thought of all the implications." This sentence shows that the thought of rape did come to mind, but the actual words used by the writer of the entry suggest that while the term came to mind, it was never fully experienced as a responsible thought. It is as if some irrational libidinal force held the thought at arm's length.

His slowness to identify his friends' act as rape is something symptomatic. The "game" played by these middle-class, fraternity boys was rape. The writer is aware of this judgment but cannot quite think it in a direct and responsible way. The word *rape* is introduced by a defensive sentence, "I mean, my friends aren't rapists," and the sentence that suggests rape is concluded by another defensive and problematic claim, "I guess their drives are just the same as everyone's." What is stated is an irrational belief, "My friends aren't rapists," that is defended by a set of shy assertions, "I guess their drives are just the same," that never focus on the central moral issues of the story.

In order to see the action of the friends as bad, the student must come to see his friends and the victim differently. This possibility for thought is introduced, the writer suggests, when he says that he "thought of all the implications of their actions." Here is a crucial point: What does it mean to think of the implications of an action? Teachers generally consider thoughts as events that can be handed from teacher to student as a material object, such as an apple. If teachers state their thoughts, students should be able to think that thought, but this is not the case. Teachers can force students to repeat the verbalization of a sentence, but they cannot force students to experience the meaning of a thought personally. Walter Freeman, in a neurobiological account of the mind, observes:

> Meanings have no edges or compartments. They are not solely rational
> or emotional, but a mixture. They are not thoughts or beliefs, but the
> fabric of both. Each meaning has a focus at some point in the dynamic
> structure of an entire life. (18)

In emphasizing a meaning's *focus* within the dynamic structure of an entire life, Freeman calls attention to meaning as force with the potential to
reshape the dynamic structure of the self. But this reshaping takes place
only when the meaning is grounded in reason and emotion, and thus it can
have an effect on the entire libidinal network of subjectivity.

Evaluative thoughts imply judgments of good and bad. This judgment is
a judgment on the worth of the ego, and it requires reformulations of libidinal attachments. These changes in attachment do not take place easily
or in the instant of a moment. They require complicated and painful shifts
in representation, the kind of shifts that I describe in my discussion of
mourning. How, then, has Berman's student come to desire to do this?

In chapter 3, I argued that students must be allowed the freedom to express their feelings, to discover their feelings as their own rather than as
something forced on them by an authority. In this case, a student has expressed his feelings and another student has been critical of these feelings. This is a point at which the development of a dialectic of desire often
reaches a critical impasse in most classes. Two students argue, and their
argument becomes an occasion for people to take sides in an argument.
The end result is too often demarcated trenches where opposite sides find
comfort in having both allies and enemies.

Arguments can be very useful in many contexts, but to stimulate real
dialectic they must be used carefully. Teaching involves a paradox. Any
time there is no conflict, there is no growth. If self-expression is merely an
opportunity for the expression of desire, there will be little opportunity for
a student to grow into a less defensive subjective posture. If, on the other
hand, there is an overly quick criticism of desire, there is a great chance
that the student will simply learn to be more defensive. How then do critical responses allow for the dialectic of mourning? What does Berman do
that many other teachers of personal writing do not do? What does he do
that many politically engaged teachers do not do?

First, I think, he provides a space where students can express honestly
what they feel. Berman allows the feelings expressed by journal writing to
lead to a productive silence. Maryanne Hannan's afterword describes how
the process works:

> He [Berman] reads five diaries selected from the thirty to forty available.
> He reads them aloud to the class, solemnly. Neither he nor members of

the class comment on the content of the diaries. When he is finished reading his selections, he returns all the diaries, including the ones he has just read, unobtrusively reincorporated into the pile. Students, anxiously casual, scan his comments and hastily put their diaries away. Jeff then collects a new set of diaries and, with sudden animation, initiates discussion of the literature assigned for that class. So it cycles, week after week, until semester's end.

Berman's solemn reading and pattern of not responding to entries read make it possible to open up a space for the subjectivity of the writer and reader that is not available in classrooms overly eager to make sense of, or judge, human experience. There is, then, at the moment of these most difficult of all negotiations of the inner self, the safety of silence.

By quoting extensively from the work of Jeffrey Berman, I do not intend to suggest that journal writing, with its dialectic of expression and silence, provides the magic key for social change and personal growth. I do not myself use journals often, though I consider them valuable. Teachers must work with their own talents to engage students in difficult tasks of thought. What Berman's example offers is a sharp insight into how emotion works as students seek to understand themselves better.

When we work with students we must not only respect what they say but we must also respect their silence, give them the freedom to be expressive in silence, and find in silence their own purchase on a discourse about to be born. In *Negation, Subjectivity, and the History of Rhetoric,* Vitanza explains Lyotard's concept of the differend to call attention to new knowledge that can emerge in this crucial moment of the pregnant unthought of thought: "The concept of differend becomes for Lyotard . . . 'the unstable state and instant of language wherein something must be able to be put into phrases cannot yet be.' He writes: 'This state includes silence.' But not the silence of forgetting" (41). Lyotard argues that the state of silence is usually marked by feeling. This feeling has some content, but that content cannot find itself in words. Yet if we, as teachers, rush this moment, we take away students' ability to find words, to find themselves, and to find their own feelings in words. We must learn, Vitanza suggests, to make "the feeling hold precedent over the argument" (41). Too often, as teachers, we find in the student's silence, our own opportunity to win an argument. When we silence our opponent, we experience victory. Such desires and assumptions about what constitutes success need to change. Berman's teaching makes another different use of silence and ensures that the teacher's desire to play the role of the master is curbed.

Berman's teaching makes effective use of silence. First, he allows writers to discover their feelings in complex relations to the other feelings within a community. Feelings are not, as in the case of demand, formed by repression. Second, however, Berman finds a way to place the student's honest expression in dialogue with other voices charged with emotion. It is this real encounter between a real personal feeling within the self and real personal feeling within another that is so hard to facilitate. Normally, we identify with others as we identify with their feelings, or we reject the feelings of another in an act of denial. Berman, in contrast, opens up a space where opposing anxious thoughts can find some meeting place in meaning. He does not allow critical responses to develop into active, fully engaged debates that simply sharpen defensive functions.

A student in a later book by Berman, *Risky Writing,* writes, "This is a class of imagination and free thought. This is a class free of criticism, except for an occasional grammatical reminder. The pressure is purely self-induced" (64). Instead of developing argumentation, Berman finds ways to encourage empathy between students who might otherwise have little concern for each other. There develops, then, among students with very different values, a sense of community. Berman writes:

> Introspective diary writing heightens the intersubjective nature of education. The connection students feel toward their teachers and class-mates offsets much of the loneliness, alienation, and depersonalization associated with the college years. Writing and listening promote students' attachment between self and other, increasing their empathic understanding and enabling them to realize the commonality of their daily lives. The development of community is one of the most valuable by-products of diary writing. (229)

Berman's graduate student, who wrote an independent afterword to the book, quoted a student diarist who said about the writing, "You suddenly realize you are not all alone" (243). In *Risky Writing,* one of Berman's students wrote, "By the nature of this class, we became connected to one another" (64).

It seems to me that the students in Berman's classes do benefit from personal development. This growth occurs, but Berman makes it clear that he is not "practicing psychotherapy" in his classes. He is simply encouraging students to "engage in self-discovery" (242). This adventure in self-discovery is not, however, simply a happy trip. The second part of Berman's title, "Pain and Growth in the Classroom," emphasizes the suffering that writers must face if they are to grow. Indeed, many of the entries show that self-discovery in Berman's diaries is generally painful. One woman wrote,

"Seeing the truth about myself is very painful because I have lived in a fantasy life for so long. I was never able to deal with the pain of life from an early age, so to protect myself I made up an imaginary world in my head" (173). If mourning means the withdrawal of libido from a fantasy world and feeling the pain of this loss of self, this student, who sees the truth about herself, has learned to mourn.

6 Conclusion

Berman's success in teaching is very much related to his ability to manage students' defensive responses as those responses are mobilized by the thoughts they encounter as they write in a social context. Berman says, "As a rule I do not read a diary aloud if it might make either the diarist or another student in the class feel defensive" (202). If the argument I have made about the ego as a defense structure is true, this offhand observation may be crucial. Berman is able to draw students into dealing with difficult issues because he knows how to avoid the defensive responses that would undermine the work of mourning necessary for their emotional progress. If we read Berman's *Diaries to an English Professor* and then follow up with Murray's account of the writing process, we can imagine how courses concerned with the political can make beneficial use of personal experience. The most important goal, here, is to develop a dialectic that engages difficult material but does not reinforce the defensive rigidity of the ego.

Mark Bracher, in *The Writing Cure*, offers useful advice on how this course would operate:

> The teacher will . . . avoid prescription, suggestion, and authoritative
> pronouncements and limit [her]self to punctuating the student's own
> discourse, returning, as Lacan put it, the subject's own message in such
> a way that the subject can recognize the heretofore unconscious desire
> contained within it. (163)

I have argued that unconscious desire is not a knowledge that can be learned in some straightforward manner. Unconscious desire is always in conflict with conscious desire. The introduction of such desire is painful because it requires modifications in a body of knowledge that support the psychic body of the self. If we remember that the self is most essentially the effect of structures of signification, we can appreciate why certain kinds of knowledge become caught in all the symptomatic practices that human subjects manifest.

If this is true, then the primary purpose for a composition course, even when it seeks political change, is not simply to teach political truths. Rather than promoting particular political beliefs, we must explore how desire supports beliefs and how the ability to be fully responsive to the ideas and real feelings of others requires slow adjustments in bodily feeling. This learning about desire and belief can work in two ways. First, we can teach that some of our beliefs, which often cause suffering to others, are resistant to dialectic. In this case, we do not need to attack the resistance we may find in our students (or ourselves); we need only review those examples that show how characteristic it is for people to dismiss beliefs that challenge their own worldviews. If we can make the failure to engage in dialectical discussion a clearly recognized failure in social responsibility, rather than an act of strength, we can begin to reclaim public discourse as a sphere for political development.

Too often, we allow public figures to dodge key issues and ignore pertinent questions. By instinct, almost, many of us admire public figures who, with commanding self-confidence, dismiss an important question with the sheer force of contempt. This kind of response, however, always plays directly into the ideological power of the master who, rather that working to make desire circulate in public discourse, works to clone and put into circulation the imperialism of his own desire.

It seems to me that the introduction of Freudian concepts has, in my lifetime, changed the rules that Americans follow in their private and public speech. My children follow their peers in talking about individuals who are "in a state of denial." This description of a certain irrational rigidity in the ability to respond to change now creates a different social and discursive world than the one inhabited by my parent's generation. People in authority are less likely to be persuasive when they seek to impose their states of denial on others. When they seek to impose such beliefs on others, people more readily see through their motives. The condition of being resistant to dialectic is not so obvious as the state of denial, but this condition might be made much more visible if composition courses began to work with dialectic seriously as a key element of discourse growth.

The Milgram experiment shows how many questions are answered simply in terms of demand. Demand frequently operates effectively to silence a question, but this kind of response needs to be recognized as a logical paradox. Demand is characteristically unresponsive to dialectic and yet is often persuasive. In the Milgram experiment, the student asked to administer a lethal shock often questions the teacher. In one striking example, Milgram records the pleas of one subject, "Must I go on? Oh, I'm worried about him. Are we going all the way up there (pointing to the higher end of the generator)? Can we stop? I'm shaking. I'm shaking. Do I have to go up there?" (80). Another woman asks, "What if there's something wrong with the man, sir?" (78). And a male subject says, "I can't stand it. I'm not going to kill that man in there. You hear him hollering?" (73). In relation to all these hesitant assertions and questions, the teacher has clear and confident responses that do not answer the question but silence the generation of questions. The experimenter responds with demands such as, "It is absolutely essential that you continue," (74) or, "The experiment must continue." No reason is given for why the experiment must continue. There is no attempt to work out an understanding of who suffers and who profits from the continuation. Instead, there is simple obedience.

Foucault has now, in some ways, made it easier for us to explore the question of who suffers and who profits from any human activity. Yet while we have neat logical formulas for exploring these issues, we fail to appreciate the emotional work necessary to bring these discourse operations into action.

Milgram wrote in a context in which the concept of obedience implied an organization with a hierarchy like that of the military. Workers in this context are like soldiers because they give up their personal identities in submission to those in authority. In our current academic climate, this kind of hierarchy is enormously suspect, but I argue that is not at all absent from real practice. Whenever we find social groups with militant leaders and close-knit followers, we find places where desire circulates as demand. In these cases, the workings of the master are often not easily detected because there is no obvious institutional hierarchy. Additionally, the master's force often operates simply as a kind of teaching, and followers may experience this teaching as a direct expression of truth. But this truth is produced, as in the Milgram experiment, by the followers' love for the master. Within their own social group, these people are relatively happy. They, however, are typically uncomfortable with outsiders, who they often see as threats to their way of life.

Milgram's work alerted Americans in the 1960s to the perils of obedience. But obedience is not simply a function of institutional authority. It is a function, as well, of disciplinary love of all kinds. On the surface, teaching always seems the opposite of military training, but whenever questions are silenced by simple assertions that defeat dialectical production, the kind of training needed to promote democratic action is subverted.

The promotion of democratic forms of discourse must be promoted. We must do more research to understand how such discourse operates. First, we can teach as a knowledge in our course, a review, of dialectic and nondialectical processes. There is an enormous amount of material that teachers can use, and I will offer only a quick sampling of material that is available.

Some scholars argue that the new electronic community offers possibilities of discourse that were not possible in the age of print media.[1] In this new community, students are free to try out different identities, to respond to the ideas of others spontaneously and quickly. While I admire the opportunity for spontaneity offered by the electronic community, I worry that it is precisely the kind of forum for writing and thought that pretends that freedom can operate without a confrontation with repression and limitation.

Postcolonial theory, especially the work of Homi Bhabha, examines how repression and various repressive binary dialectics maintain Western stereotypes. Bhabha also explores how new discourses can work against this imperialism. He suggests that the work of Cornel West,

> represents a logic of living that cuts across the everyday life of different
> ideological forms—race, religion, patriarchy, homophobia; it reveals,
> and contests, the mechanisms by which self-images and self-identities
> are formed in the realm of cultural styles, aesthetic ideals, psychosexual
> sensibilities. (230)

Postcolonial perspectives also offer useful perspectives on dialectic and social communities. A character in Rosa Shand's *The Gravity of Sunlight* explores the differing discourse habits of the peoples of Uganda:

> In Lagno and Acholi and West Nile, you have Nilotic peoples. The
> tribal organization of Nilotic groups is relatively democratic. That is,
> the males sit around and decide things by consensus. The people display
> a fresh straight-forwardness. The kingdoms of the south, however—
> Bunyoro and Buganda and farther afield, Ruanda . . . were never demo-
> cratic in their structure. Theirs is a rigid hierarchy. These are the people
> that the British understood. (106)

In the West, the history of rhetoric has complex examples of figures who have promoted dialectic and democracy. Socrates is perhaps the most famous for having insisted on a form of questioning that simply followed a desire for truth. Having injured the sensibilities of many of the citizens of Athens through his questioning, however, Socrates was silenced. Roman rhetoric adopted many of the same values of Greek rhetoric but had a precarious existence. Cicero wrote many works on rhetoric but is reported to have considered killing Julius Caesar after a particularly damaging confrontation with him in the senate. As a theorist, Cicero argued that dialectical questioning was key to resolving disputes. Stasis theory developed, in part, from Cicero's attempt to formulate an approach to establish truth through the pursuit of dialectical questions. In *De Inventione*, he writes,

"Every subject which contains in itself a controversy to be resolved by speech and debate involves a question about a fact, or about definition, or about the nature of an act, or about legal processes" (1.10). In Cicero's view, any controversy can work toward a resolution through the pursuit of questions that systematically seek to establish the truth of various kinds of propositions. Many composition teachers today use stasis theory as a mode for developing persuasive arguments.

Any course that features a positive account of dialectical development in the classical world should include a more realistic view of the many misdirections of dialectic. Jean-Francois Lyotard, in *The Differend: Phrases in Dispute*, and Victor Vitanza and D. Diane Davis, who respond to these ideas, offer subtle commentary on the function of dialectic. Deborah Tannen has an excellent chapter on asking questions in her book *That's Not What I Meant: How Conversational Style Makes or Breaks Relationships*, showing how some families delight in asking questions while others feel insulted and interrogated. Tannen's work indicates very strongly that work on dialectic needs to be very attentive to the implicit, not simply the explicit, messages involved.

If I have suggested that resistance to dialectic is something that we can easily teach as knowledge, dialectic itself, as a mode for the circulation of desire, is not easily taught or practiced. Tannen shows that any simple formula asking for logical questions is often secondary to the real work of circulating understanding. The give and take of discussion does not work on some logical basis but on generally invisible signals. She observes:

> These are some typical ways the conversational signals of pacing, pausing, loudness, and pitch are used to carry on the business of taking turns in conversation; relating ideas to each other and showing what the point is; and showing how we feel about what we're saying and the person we're saying it to. . . . These conversation signals and devices are normally invisible, the silent and hidden gears that drive conversations. We don't pay attention to the gears unless something seems to have gone wrong. (61)

We can easily show examples of failures in dialectic. I have quoted clear examples from both Žižek and Milgram, and it is easy to show how these failures can lead to violence. It is more difficult to represent how discourse dialectic can actually work. Tannen argues that communication between people of goodwill is fraught with great potential for unintentional insult and irritation.

Tannen gives an interesting example of how nondialectical forms of conversation can proceed, just skirting the fringes of direct and hostile confrontation. She was invited to discuss an article she had written on the New York conversational style by a celebrity talk-show host. The talk-show host tried to discuss Tannen's work with her but found it difficult to accept Tannen's central claim about the relative ethics of interrupting a conversation. Tannen describes the discussion thus:

> When I said that my research proves that people can indeed talk and listen at the same time, she said, "It's just not polite. There are no manners considered here, are there?" In response to this, I offered a discourse on the relativity of concepts of politeness, in the course of which I began to say, "You may not think it's polite. . . . " The host cut in at that point and said, "I don't. I absolutely don't," and soon moved on to ask, "But what is it about a New Yorker's vocabulary?"
>
> Our conversation proceeded in this way. I never managed to convince my host of the cultural relativity of politeness. At the end of the show, she thanked me for being her guest and told the listening audience, "If you talk like that—any one of you—I'll be very angry!" And that was the last word. (188)

Tannen generally seeks to avoid any psychological analysis of discourse, but it is easy to see this discussion as a confrontation of power that generates various defenses in order to avoid any dialectic that shares power. Tannen's host interrupts in order to assert a paradoxical belief demand: Interruptions show a basic lack of manners. The host, who calls interruptions bad manners, shows her bad manners in order to insist on her claim that people not show bad manners.

Insult and irritation are often just below the surface of a flow of discourse in which two people compete to establish credibility. The very ability to establish some common ground for collecting and evaluating evidence is made impossible as the result of hurt feelings. Objectively, I imagine, someone who believes that there are basic structures for manners would find it interesting to discover that such a belief might not be true. Such an expression of desire to know could have shifted this discussion into the traditional safe discourse of the university. Another safe pathway for the development of the dialectic would be to explore, or even argue about, how one would establish evidence for such a claim. But these potential pathways for the development of interest (mobilization of desire) fail to materialize, as they often do in everyday affairs. They are the kind of failures we take for granted. It seems to me, however, that these accepted failures are things we can change when we better understand how to teach people why it is important to want and expect such changes.

The feelings of insult and irritation generated in encounters, such as those Tannen describes, are forms of bodily pain that result from ego attachments. In theory, we can all live happily in discourse if we simply learn to give up our egos. In fact, much of contemporary theory endorses just that, the abandonment of personal forms of identity. But the very ideal of giving up an ego often becomes a hypocritical belief system used to discriminate between good people and bad, and thus carries on the violence associated with ego positions. Giving up attachments to the ego involves not simply the action of a belief, as we find in thought, but also the work of mourning. For all people, this work is never finished, though it may be that some people work better at it than others. The real work of giving up the ego is an effect of the work of libidinal withdrawal, of mourning. When we begin to consider seriously how this work is not the accomplishment of a simple act of thought but a painful process of symbolic flexibility, when we begin to understand how we can help ourselves and others do this work, we may be able to do better work in composition classes.

Notes

1. Introduction

1. Another useful perspective on attachments (though not at all compatible with Lacanian thought) is offered by John Bowlby and his work on attachment theory. From this perspective, the human subject is essentially an attachment structure. While Bowlby was much admired in the 1950s, his work was also regarded with deep suspicion because it challenged many essential psychoanalytic concepts. More recently, a number of prominent clinicians—Susie Orbach in "Why Is Attachment in the Air?," and Stephen Mitchell in "Attachment Theory and the Psychoanalytic Tradition: Reflections on Human Relationality"—have sought to bring attachment theory into mainstream clinical reflection.

2. Horowitz seeks to make sense of the forces that instigate such riots.

3. Problems of community, identity, solidarity, oppression, and exclusion have been well discussed by scholars. Kaja Silverman, in *Male Subjectivity at the Margins,* and Diana Fuss, in *Identification Papers,* explore what it might mean to establish identities that dismantle destructive ideologies. Chantal Mouffe's concept of *agonistic pluralism,* in "Deliberative Democracy or Agonistic Pluralism," seeks to describe a community of individuals who engage in public discourse and share freedom and equality but do not demand forms of identification that exclude others. D. Diane Davis, in "Addicted to Love; Or, Toward an Inessential Solidarity," offers an excellent discussion of these issues for scholars of rhetoric. As a corrective to Mouffe's *common political identity,* Davis endorses what she terms a *disidentifying (postmodernist-Vitanzan) rhetoric.* In the course of this book, I endorse this argument, but I also try to show how it requires a work of mourning, a work on the libidinal fabric of the self.

2. The Subject in Postmodernist Theory: Discourse, Ideology, and Therapy in the Classroom

1. David Reider in a paper, "The Subject of Change: Goran Therborn or Jacques Lacan," published with Victor Vitanza's Research Network Forum, argues that Berlin was not likely to have been led to a Lacanian model of subjectivity.

2. Judith Butler in *Contingency, Hegemony, Universality,* observes:

> Why any of us stay in situations that are manifestly inimical to our interests, and why our collective interests are so difficult to know—or indeed to remember—is not easy to determine. It seems clear, however, that we will not begin to determine it without a psychoanalytic perspective. (149)

3. On Unfree Speech and the Pedagogy of Demand

1. Boyd discusses resistance in relation to older forms of traditional rhetoric, as a response to the political aspirations of scholars such as Richard Ohman, Colleen Tremonte, and Ira Shor, and as a dimension of the psychological concerns of scholars such as Lad Tobin and Robert Brooke.

2. Hairston documents a widespread support of politicized teaching in composition work. She quotes from Charles Paine's *College English* article in which Paine asserts, "the teacher must recognize that he or she must influence (perhaps manipulate is the more accurate word) students' values through charisma or power—he or she must accept the role as manipulator" (564). Hairston (responding to another author supporting "confrontational" relations with students) argues, "Distressingly often, those who advocate such courses show open contempt for the students' values, preferences, or interests" (24).

3. Don H. Bialostosky's essay, in Harkin and Schilb's *Contending with Words: Composition and Rhetoric in a Postmodern Age,* did an effective job of emphasizing the importance of Bakhtin to composition theorists. Numerous books and essays have appeared to integrate Bakhtin within composition theory. Helen Rothschild Ewald's "Waiting for Answerability: Bakhtin and Composition Studies," stresses the ethical dimension of Bakhtin's concept of dialogue. Jeffrey T. Nealon, in "The Ethics of Dialogue: Bakhtin and Levinas," offers a good discussion of the relations between self and other in Bakhtin. My own sense, however, is that Bakhtin's dialogic account of desire currently seems to have less support than Foucault's and, more recently, Judith Butler's account of desire as subjection.

4. D. Diane Davis, in "Addicted to Love; Or, Toward an Inessential Solidarity," develops a useful argument about the addiction to love as a problem in the formation of community. Davis's suggestion that addiction can "set the course . . . perhaps at the level of drive" resembles the argument I develop in chapter 4.

5. Joseph H. Smith, in *Arguing with Lacan: Ego Psychology and Language,* offers a useful analysis on relations among affect, repression, and consciousness in a section on affective recognition. "Affective recognition," Smith suggests, is "a shorthand way of talking about any real recognition as opposed to some intellectualized, relatively affectless, obsessional chain of signifiers" (87). "One's basic conscious attunement to inner and outer world is thus mediated by affect and is lived out as one's dominant mood" (86).

6. I do not intend to suggest here a promotion of free trade or capitalism. Capitalism is often not democratic in practice even when it promotes freedom as an ideological ruse.

7. Alan France, in "Dialectics of Self: Structure and Agency as the Subject of English," advocates what he calls a *posthumanist* and *post-Foucauldian* pedagogy that would allow students "to assemble and assimilate the fragments of postmodern experience into a coherent, self-conscious identity in order to communicate, or to join discourse communities" (145–65).

8. Gilbert D. Chaitin, in *Rhetoric and Culture in Lacan,* quotes Lacan to suggest that this interplay between child and mother, "forms part of that primitive symbolization which precedes language" (169).

9. Generally, we might assume that the teacher becomes the Other as a general effect of projection. Societies, to various degrees, encourage these expectations and projections. In reality, various unconscious cues regarding anxiety and desire will trigger different degrees and different forms of projection. Both the teacher and the student play a role in determining how these projections have effects and the extent to which the teacher will play the role of the Other for the student.

4. Desire as Agency:
The Ethics and Politics of Composition

1. Judith Butler remarks in *The Psychic Life of Power,* "The value of psychoanalysis is . . . to be found in a consideration of how identification and its failures are crucial to the thinking of hegemony" (149).

2. For an excellent discussion of the importance and difficulties of moving beyond an essentially "dyadic" relation with one parent, see John Muller, *Beyond the Psychoanalytic Dyad: Developmental Semiotics in Freud, Pierce, and Lacan.*

3. I would hope that the old argument regarding whether there are individualized desires has been put to rest. As a short argument, I suggest that personal desires are, of course, nothing more than social desires that have become attached to us. For a more complex argument, see my *Narcissism and the Literary Libido.*

4. Fred Alford, in *Group Psychology and Political Theory,* makes a compelling case for the human need for masters. Masters are needed for human society to function, but as Alford points out in "Interpretive Leadership and the Charms of Corruption," some forms of leaderships can help followers develop more independent, anti-ideological styles of thought.

5. David Metzger, in *The Lost Cause of Rhetoric: The Relation of Rhetoric and Geometry in Aristotle and Lacan,* offers a useful discussion of the four discourses in relation to Aristotle and time. Metzger argues that "rhetoric consists of what has dropped out of the symbolization of each of those genres [psychology, philosophy, ethics, or any science] of inquiry," and argues, "The relation of questions and commands requires a reading of desire" (21).

6. The *objet a* is a complicated term to define. Henry Krips emphasizes that we consider it not as some thing desired, but the "cause of desire rather than its object" (23). Pushing this argument further, we might argue that since desire is a defense against, or response to, anxiety, then anxiety is the cause of the desire. It is incorrect to equate the object with anxiety, but it is important to see that there will always be relations between anxiety and desire. Anything that signals anxiety will generate a desire to overcome anxiety, and enjoyment, in itself, is a useful defense against anxiety.

7. See Max Weber, *On Charisma and Institution Building;* Jerome A. Winer, Thomas Jobe, and Carlton Ferrono, "Toward a Psychoanalytic Theory of the Charismatic Relationship"; W. La Barre, *The Ghost Dance: Origins of Religion;* and my own *Narcissism and the Literary Libido.*

8. Enjoyment and identification are, of course, more complicated than this. It is possible that students wanting to enjoy *Ally McBeal* might watch it and not enjoy it. This is because enjoyment is always allied to anxiety and is structured primarily in relation to the Other as it functions as a dialectical partner for the ego. This Other is always projected into social space, but it is never quite the same as any particular other (real person) present in social space.

9. Asking and answering questions is also hard for academics. It is of course part of the ritual of scholarly papers to ask questions. But when "important" people give talks, there is a noticeable timidity about asking questions that might give offense. The older I get, the more I think I see cases in which powerful superstars generate in audiences an inability to experience the need for a question.

5. Engaging Affect:
Dialectic, Drive, and the Mourning of Identity

1. This is because, in *Looking Awry,* Žižek claims, "what we call reality implies the surplus of fantasy space filling out the black hole of the real" (viii).

2. Drive is an important but elusive concept for a psychoanalytic social theory because it designates a structure that acts like instinct but is determined by speech demands. Like instinct, drive speaks in terms of immediate and apparently natural, spontaneous bodily experience. Like instinct, it is deaf to speech. But though drive is experienced as

a natural response of the body, it is, in fact, a social construction. It is constructed by social interaction, by Lacan's *laws of the signifier.*

Drive is not a well-understood concept. Since the introduction of the German term *Trieb,* by Freud, drive is sometimes understood as biological and sometimes simply translated as psychic energy. My interest in the term stems from Freud's 1915 essay, "Instincts and their Vicissitudes," in which he placed drive "on the frontier between the mental and the somatic . . . the psychical representative of the stimuli originating from within the organism and reaching the mind" (121–22). Drive works as a *psychical representative* of biological processes, but it is not a direct expression of instinct or biology. Sergio Staude explains drive as "that which occurs in our bodies due the external action of the Other. The drive connects two non-homogeneous fields producing effects in both of them: the body will be a drive's body and the psychic apparatus a phantasmatic apparatus" (15). The crucial point here is the claim that drive representations produce effects in two nonhomogeneous fields. Just as mental, phantasmatic phenomena is influenced by drive, so is bodily experience influenced by mind.

Renata Salecl, in *(per)versions of love and hate,* explains, "Drive first needs to be understood as something left over after the subject becomes the subject of the signifier and is incorporated into a symbolic structure" (48). Drives are patterns of repetition caught in the body. Drives can allow a body to speak irrationally in a language of motion, sensation, or even lack of sensation. Human behavior can act out drives for sex or food, and also for love and death.

3. Lynn Worsham, responding to T. R. Johnson, in "Discipline and Pleasure: 'Magic' and Sound," argues that pleasure, in and of itself, is not an effective personal or political agenda. We must, Worsham suggests, be willing to experience thoughts that are not pleasant or pleasurable.

6. Conclusion

1. See for example Lester Faigley's *Fragments of Rationality* and Wayne Butler and James Kinneavy's "The Electronic Discourse Community: god, Meet Donald Duck."

De Man, Paul. *Blindness and Insight: Essays in the Rhetoric of Contemporary Criticism.* New York: Oxford UP, 1971.

Dews, Peter. *Logics of Disintegration: Post-structuralist Thought and the Claims of Critical Theory.* London: Verso, 1990.

Dor, Joël. *Introduction to the Reading of Lacan: The Unconscious Structured like a Language.* Ed. Judith Feher Gurewich and Susan Fairfield. Northvale, NJ: Jason Aronson, 1997.

Eagleton, Terry. *Ideology: An Introduction.* London: Verso, 1991.

Easthope, Anthony. "The Subject of Literary and the Subject of Cultural Studies." *Texts for Change: Theory, Pedagogy, Politics.* Ed. Donald Morton and Mas'ud Zavarzadeh. Urbana. U of Illinois P, 1991. 33–46.

Ebert, Teresa. "For a Red Pedagogy: Feminism, Desire, and Need." *College English* 58 (1996): 795–819.

———. *Ludic Feminism and After: Postmodernism, Desire, and Labor in Late Capitalism.* Ann Arbor: U of Michigan P, 1996.

Eisenstadt, S. N., ed. *Max Weber on Charisma and Institution Building: Selected Papers.* Chicago: U of Chicago P, 1968.

Elbow, Peter. *Writing with Power: Techniques for Mastering the Writing Process.* New York: Oxford UP, 1981.

Emig, Janet. "Writing as Mode of Learning" *College Composition and Communication* 28 (1977): 122–28.

Evans, Dylan. *A Dictionary of Lacanian Psychoanalysis.* London: Routledge, 1996.

Ewald, Helen Rothschild. "Waiting for Answerability: Bakhtin and Composition Studies." *College Composition and Communication* 44 (1993): 331–48.

Faigley, Lester. *Fragments of Rationality.* Pittsburgh: U of Pittsburgh P, 1992.

Fink, Bruce. *The Lacanian Subject: Between Language and Jouissance.* Princeton: Princeton UP, 1995.

Fish, Stanley. "There Is No Such Thing as Free Speech and It's a Good Thing Too." *Debating P.C.: The Controversy over Political Correctness on College Campuses.* Ed. Paul Berman. Laurel, NY: Dell, 1992. 231–95.

Flower, Linda. *Problem-Solving Strategies for Writing.* Fort Worth: Harcourt, 1981.

France, Alan. "Dialectics of the Self: Structure and Agency as the Subject of English." *College English* 63 (2000): 145–65.

Freeman, Walter. *How Brains Make up Their Minds.* London: Phoenix, 1999.

Freud, Sigmund. "Inhibitions, Symptoms and Anxiety." 1926. Trans. and ed. James Strachey. *The Standard Edition of Complete Psychological Works of Sigmund Freud.* Vol. 20. London: Hogarth, 1959. 77–179.

———. "Instincts and Their Vicissitudes" 1915. Trans. and ed. James Strachey. *The Standard Edition of Complete Psychological Works of Sigmund Freud.* Vol. 14. London: Hogarth, 1947. 237–58.

———. "Mourning and Melancholia." 1917. Trans. and ed. James Strachey. *The Standard Edition of Complete Psychological Works of Sigmund Freud.* Vol. 14. London: Hogarth, 1947. 237–60.

Fuss, Diana. *Identification Papers.* New York: Routledge, 1995.

Geertz, Clifford. *The Interpretation of Cultures; Selected Essays.* New York: Basic, 1973.

Guntrip, Harry. "My Experience of Analysis with Fairbairn and Winnicott." *The International Review of Psycho-Analysis* 2 (1975): 145–56.

Hairston, Maxine. "Diversity, Ideology, and the Teaching of Writing." *College Composition and Communication* 43 (1992): 179–93.

Hannan, Maryanne. Afterword. *Diaries to an English Professor: Pain and Growth in the Classroom.* By Jeffrey Berman. Amherst: U of Massachusetts P, 1994. 243–73.

Harris, Joseph. "The Course as Text/The Teacher as Critic." *College English* 55 (1993): 785–93.

Horowitz, Donald. *The Deadly Ethnic Riot.* Berkeley: U of California P, 2000.

Johnson, T. R. "Discipline and Pleasure: 'Magic' and Sound." *Journal of Advanced Composition* 19 (1999): 431–52.

Kinneavy, James. *A Theory of Discourse.* New York: Norton, 1980.

Krips, Henry. *Fetish: An Erotics of Culture.* Ithaca: Cornell UP, 1999.

La Barre, Weston. *The Ghost Dance: Origins of Religion.* New York: Delta, 1972.

Lacan, Jacques. *The Seminar of Jacques Lacan Book II: The Ego in Freud's Theory and in the Technique of Psychoanalysis 1954–1955.* Ed. Jacques-Alain Miller and John Forrester. Trans. Sylvana Tomaselli. New York: Norton, 1991.

——. *The Seminar of Jacques Lacan Book III. The Psychoses.* Ed. Jacques-Alain Miller. Trans. Russell Grigg. New York: Norton, 1993.

——. *The Seminar of Jacques Lacan Book VII. The Ethics of Psychoanalysis 1959–1960.* Ed. Jacques-Alain Miller. Trans. Sylvana Tomaselli. New York: Norton, 1988.

——. *The Seminar of Jacques Lacan Book XI. The Four Fundamental Concepts of Psychoanalysis.* Ed. Jacques-Alain Miller. Trans. Alan Sheridan. New York: Norton, 1977.

——. *The Seminar of Jacques Lacan Book XX. On Feminine Sexuality, the Limits of Love and Knowledge: Encore.* Ed. Jacques-Alain Miller. Trans. Bruce Fink. New York: Norton, 1998.

Laclau, Ernesto. *Emancipation(s).* London: Verso, 1996.

Lee, Jonathan Scott. *Jacques Lacan.* Amherst: U of Massachusetts P, 1991.

Lemaire, Anika. *Jacques Lacan.* London: Routledge, 1977.

Lindemann, Erich. "Symptomatology and Management of Acute Grief." In *Essential Papers on Object Loss.* New York: New York UP, 1994.

Lindemann, Erika. *A Rhetoric for Writing Teachers.* New York: Oxford UP, 1995.

Loewald, H. "Internalization, Separation, Mourning, and the Superego." *Psychoanalytic Quarterly* 31 (1962): 483–504.

Lunsford, Andrea, John Ruszkiewicz, and Keith Walters. *Everything's an Argument.* Boston: St. Martins, 1998.

Macdonell, Diane. *Theories of Discourse: An Introduction.* Oxford: Basil Blackwell, 1986.